THE LOVE BOOK FOR COUPLES

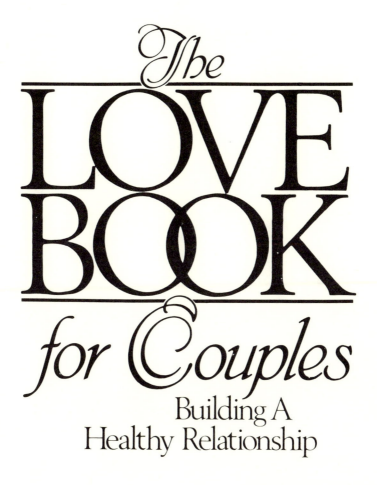

The LOVE BOOK for Couples

Building A Healthy Relationship

E. Michael Lillibridge, Ph.D.

Humanics Limited * Atlanta, Georgia

HUMANICS LIMITED
P.O. Box 7447
Atlanta, Georgia 30309

Third Printing, 1987

Library of Congress Card Catalog Number: 83 - 81431

PRINTED IN THE UNITED STATES OF AMERICA

ISBN: 0 - 89334 - 048 - 0

Acknowledgment

A special note of thanks to my father, Dr. G.D. Lillibridge, who edited and reviewed the entire manuscript prior to publication and was of immeasurable help in putting the manuscript in final copy. My deepest thanks.

E. MICHAEL LILLIBRIDGE

table of contents

introduction

Bob opened his first psychotherapy session with the upsetting disclosure that he was no longer in love with his wife. When Bob and Sue entered my office both looked very unhappy. Bob was sullen, aloof, and distant. Sue was on the verge of tears and appeared very frightened. Talking with them for an hour, I learned they were in their early thirties, had been married for eight years, and had three small children. Bob was a successful manager and sales representative. Sue was a housewife and part-time interior decorator. Both were successful in their careers. The couple was financially secure, had lovely children they cared about deeply, and appeared to have a promising life together. But over the course of the session Bob revealed that he no longer wanted to remain married; he believed he loved Sue, but was no longer *in* love with her. He said, "I feel more for her as if she was a friend, a sister, but not my wife. I don't feel I'm in love with her anymore."

Sue had run the gamut of emotions: shock, hurt, anger, panic, since Bob had broken this news to her several days before. She said she knew they were having problems, but she didn't feel they were so serious that Bob should leave home. She loved Bob and didn't want to lose him.

In taking a clinical history, I discovered that during the past year Sue felt that Bob had become cold and distant and no longer shared his feelings with her. She stated that he stayed away from the family more and more and preferred to go out with his friends rather than with her. Bob, on the other hand, said that their sex life "had gone to hell," and that Sue was unaffectionate most of the time. His primary concern, however, which had been building up for about a year, was simply that he no longer loved Sue. Now he doubted whether he wanted to go on living with someone he didn't love.

During the entire hour Bob had remained aloof and distant, Sue hurt and scared. Only on one occasion did this pattern change. When discussing their early days together, both relaxed and loosened up. Their courtship had been a

1

happy and enjoyable one. They had fallen in love shortly after meeting, enjoyed an exciting and stimulating sex life, did many fun things together (golf, tennis, skiing), and helped and supported each other in their respective careers. Clearly they had enriched each other's lives during this period. Now, several years later, they fought and argued most of the time, had little or no sex, seemed to be in warring camps. Bob was planning on leaving the marriage because he was no longer in love with Sue. What had gone wrong?

Why is it so many relationships between men and women often start out to be caring, loving, and enjoyable, and then end up creating anger, pain, and frustration, with one or both people wanting out? Why do we have so much difficulty making love relationships work successfully?

Because love relationships seem so critical to our happiness and our sense of well-being, it is important to understand what the ingredients of a successful love relationship are and what steps you can take to make your relationship with someone you love a rewarding and happy one.

This, then, is specifically a book on love, primarily for men and women who are currently involved in a love relationship (i.e. married, engaged, dating). Individuals who are not presently in such a relationship, but are divorced, widowed, or single, however, should also find many useful ideas which will help them now and also be of benefit to them when they enter into a more permanent relationship.

For the past ten years as a psychologist and marriage and family therapist, I have seen hundreds of couples and individuals who were concerned about the quality of their love relationships. People come for help asking why they fell in love with a particular person or why they fell out of love. Couples often can't communicate with one another, but they don't know why. Some are concerned about how to make their relationship a better and more satisfying one. Some say they love each other, but can't get along on a day-to-day basis. Still others wonder why the *feeling* of love has diminished over time and how they can recapture that "falling in love" feeling.

The problem for all such people seems to be, "What is love and how can I have a successful love relationship that will last?"

Couples often think that "falling in love" is enough, that this feeling of love will hold them together forever and through thick and thin. In reality, most people have little knowledge about the makeup of this kind of relationship and what knowledge and skills are needed to maintain a satisfying relationship.

The purpose of this book is to provide couples with the skills which will help them to improve their love relationships. If couples are to stay in love and be happy with each other, they must understand three important areas of relating to each other.

PART ONE/
How to Build a Healthy Relationship

The first area explored in this book deals with six aspects of couple relationships that need to be understood and experienced if a happy relationship is to be achieved. First, we will examine the *feeling of love* that is so important to a relationship. We will explore why an individual falls in love with one person as opposed to another, what romantic love is as compared to mature love, and how these feeling of love that occur early in the development of a relationship can be maintained and revitalized. Next, we will deal with two important *interpersonal skills*, giving and assertion, that couples need to possess so that they can meet both their own and their loved ones' needs. Following this, we will deal with a critical factor for all couples: achieving *sexual compatibility*. We will see how men and women are different in the conditions that make them sexual. Understanding this difference and taking specific steps that acknowledge these differences is the key to achieving sexual harmony. Then we will explore *interpersonal conflicts*, and focus on how couples can learn to fight fairly and honestly with each other. All couples argue and disagree. The secret to resolving such disputes is finding effective methods of resolving their differences so that both win. Then we will look at the concept of *emotional intimacy*, which focuses on how to develop deep, caring, loving feelings for your partner. We will discuss specific skills that help couples to draw closer to one another: learning to listen, genuine self-disclosure, and the importance of giving. Finally, we will examine the need all couples have to spend *positive, enjoyable time* together and to find pleasure and good times in each other's company. As a consequence of such good times, their relationship is enriched and they enjoy their lives more.

These six aspects of couple relationships are very interdependent: the more successful couples are in one aspect, the more likely they will be successful in another. For example, when they resolve their conflicts democratically and there are no leftover hurt, angry, and bitter feelings, then the chances are that their sex lives and feelings of love will be positive. If, on the other hand, they can't solve their differences and are chronically angry with one another, they're usually not too sexually attracted to each other nor do they have loving feelings. So, couples need to be successful in all six of these aspects of relationship to insure a more harmonious relationship with each other.

3

PART TWO/Neurotic Love Relationships

In the second part of this book we will note that the failure to meet one or more of the above six elements in a healthy relationship often leads to the development of self-defeating relationships. The basic dynamics of the self-defeating love relationship involve an unequal balance of power between partners and a drift into rigid, inflexible role-playing with one another. We will explore in detail three common types of self-defeating relationships: the angry versus the appeasing partner, the over-protective versus the helpless partner, and the nagging versus the irresponsible partner. Then we will examine what specific steps can be taken to change each type of relationship into a happier, productive one.

PART THREE/Enriching the Love Relationship via Self-Love

The last area of exploration centers on the basic things we can do by ourselves to insure the likelihood of a successful relationship. While the first two areas discuss things couples can do together, this last area involves dealing with yourself as an individual. In the broadest sense, you can do the most to insure a successful love relationship by first learning to love and accept yourself as a human being. You can learn to do this in two ways: by meeting your basic psychological needs and by enriching your self-esteem. The basic psychological needs involve relating effectively to other people, becoming your own person, being able to achieve and be successful at something, and having the capacity for fun and pleasure in your life. After examining how to meet these psychological needs, we will explore specifically how to enhance self-esteem, including the positive steps needed to increase feelings of self-worth. When individuals begin truly to accept and love themselves, it becomes easier to develop and maintain a healthy love relationship with a member of the opposite sex.

This book has been written in a simple, down-to-earth manner. The goal is not only to provide you with a blueprint for evaluating yourself in your love relationship, but also to give you concrete ideas and specific suggestions for making your love life more viable and exciting.

PART ONE

How to Build a Healthy Love Relationship

1

the feeling of love

You meet someone at a party and after talking for several minutes you find you are really attracted to this other person. Usually, this is not just a sexual attraction, although for most people that element is definitely there. Rather, it's that you feel this person could be the right one for you, your perfect match. As a result, you're turned on and stimulated by being with him or her. You want to put your best foot forward. You want to make a good impression. And you very much want this person to like you. The feelings you are experiencing are the beginning of what we call romantic love. Although it should be pointed out that not all love relationships need begin this way, most people have probably had this very real and exciting experience at one time or another. We're going to begin our exploration of how couples can become more loving by understanding the phenomena of romantic love.

the high of romantic love

In this chapter we will deal with the feeling of romantic love: that exciting feeling you have when you first get involved with someone you are attracted to. Everyone has probably had this experience of "falling in love" at some point in life. It is a wonderful feeling — a real high! During its presence you are totally oblivious to all else. Work, school, responsibilities mean little to you. It's easy to ignore your commitments and obligations. When you are not with

7

the other person, you're constantly thinking and daydreaming about him or her. When you're together, no matter what you do is fun and exciting — even if it involves just sitting and staring dreamily into each other's eyes. Romantic love is fun and makes you glad to be alive. After the onset of adolescence it can occur at any age. Eighty-year-old people can fall in love and do all the "mushy" things teenagers are accused of doing when in love. Hollywood and the media often "hype" romantic love. We have all seen the B movie where boy gets girl — they kiss passionately and go off into the sunset to live happily ever after in a perpetual glow of romantic love. But can Romantic Love really last forever?

three stages of love

It would be wonderful if Romantic Love lasted forever. If it did, probably little work would ever get done in this world, but life would be fabulous. Unfortunately, Romantic Love does not last forever. Relationships can start in several ways, such as being friends, acquaintances, even enemies, and also by "falling in love". Once a couple has fallen in love, however, they tend to go through a rather predictable sequence of steps. In fact, there are usually three discernable stages to being in love with someone. The first is Romantic Love, the head-over-heels kind of love that makes you feel fantastic. This stage usually lasts three to six months before it starts to wear off. Then the paragon of perfection you have been passionately in love with starts to change.

This leads to the second stage, that of Disappointment/Disillusionment. During this stage, which lasts several months or more, you begin to notice all the faults and foibles of this "perfect person" which somehow escaped your attention before. That little personality trait that was once cute and sweet now becomes irksome and annoying. At first, when you enter this stage, you are often surprised and confused by these new-found and unpleasant "revelations" about your loved one. Surprise and confusion often give way to anger and resentment, for your loved one is no longer living up to your expectations. Usually you then try to change your beloved back towards your fantasy expectations; this attempt leads to many arguments and conflicts. Often, for the first time in the relationship, couples are openly angry and fight and argue with each other. When they realize their loved one can't or won't change, that he or she is not now and cannot be the perfect person, anger turns to disappointment and, at times, disillusionment. This is a low point in the love relationship and many relationships end here because the couple cannot live with their differences. Many, if not most, relationships survive this difficult time, however, and individuals begin to accept their loved ones on more realistic terms.

This change leads to the third stage: Mature Love. In Mature Love you accept the whole person — strengths and assets, faults and foibles. Mature Love grows and deepens over time as you come to know your loved one in deeper and more meaningful ways. The constant high of Romantic Love is gone, but it is replaced with a deeper caring and concern for the whole person. Romantic Love is, in many ways, a kind of narcissistic love — your real concern is yourself. In Romantic Love you may give gifts, favors, time and attention to your loved one, but what you really want is for this person to fulfill your unrealistic expectations of the perfect mate. How nice for you! In Mature Love you learn to give and care, and the welfare of someone else becomes significant to you. You now appreciate your beloved as a person and not just as a love object to satisfy your needs. While Romantic Love and Disillusionment are relatively brief in time, Mature Love can last a lifetime if you nurture it and work hard to maintain it. In subsequent chapters we shall see how this is done. These, then, are the three rather common and predictable stages of love.

why do we fall in love with one person as opposed to another?

Knowing that falling in love (Romantic Love) is different than being in love (Mature Love) can help you understand better your feelings for someone. But why do people fall in love with one person rather than another? Is it just fate, or do individuals consciously choose those they fall in love with? If you talk to those experiencing Romantic Love, they will often tell you it was fate that brought them together. But if you discuss the choice of a loved one with those who are in Mature Love, they will usually give more concrete reasons why they picked their mates or their loved ones over someone else.

Falling in love with a specific person is no accident. Everyone has a definition of what constitutes the ideal mate. Everyone has a set of criteria as to what is desirable in a spouse or a loved one. This list of criteria is made up of things that people are consciously aware of, but also things they are unaware of. For example, a man says to himself that he wants a woman who is attractive, outgoing, wants to stay at home and raise children, and is highly affectionate. If he meets a woman who matches this set of criteria, chances are he will be very attracted to her and, all things being equal, he could fall in love with her. Likewise a woman could desire a man who is a professional, rich, attractive, and athletic. If she finds a man who matches a significant number of the items on her list she, too, will likely fall in love with him. When two people get together and each matches the other's list of criteria, there is the beginning of a love relationship. You fall in love then with someone because

9

that individual meets your needs or you anticipate that he or she will.

People also tend to choose individuals who not only meet their conscious needs, but are a reflection of what people think of themselves. This aspect of mate selection is one that few people are consciously aware of. If, for example, you have a healthy self-concept and feel good about yourself, you tend to pick someone who will also feel good about you and respect you as a person. If, on the other had, you don't have a positive self-concept but possess negative or guilty feelings about yourself (conscious or unconscious), you will often pick a mate whose attitude towards you reflects your own attitude towards yourself. So, if you are verbally abused, put down, or treated poorly on a consistent basis by someone you love, it may reflect the fact that you don't feel good about yourself. In short, you may believe you deserve the negative behavior you are getting from your partner. The old saying fits to some degree: "If you feel like a loser, people will treat you like a loser." The opposite is also true, however: if you generally feel like a winner, people tend to treat you with the respect you give yourself. Whether your self-image is basically positive or negative, it becomes perpetuated over time because others tend to treat you as you treat yourself. As a result, sometimes people may choose a person with the opposite traits of those they think they want. But the traits they are choosing are consistent with their underlying self-concept.

Thus, the selection of mates is usually not accidental but a personal reflection of conscious and unconscious values and ideals desired in a mate.

why do we fall out of love?

If you fall in love because someone meets your needs ("the criteria list"), you can fall out of love because those needs are no longer being met. If you fall in love because someone is rich and attractive, then if the money and good looks go you could fall out of love. People fall out of love because others change or they change. If you change, you have changed the list of criteria important to you. For example, suppose you married someone because that individual is attractive, athletic, carefree and sexy. As time went on, however, suppose you found communication, emotional closeness, and commitment even more important than good looks and a carefree attitude. Then you could fall out of love even though your partner has not changed. Your partner is still carefree, attractive and sexy, but lacks the new qualities you now value more.

You could also fall out of love because your partner has changed. For instance, a husband married his wife in part because she would stay at home and raise the children, be somewhat dependent on him (financially and emotionally), and allow him to be the major decision-maker in the home. After the children are raised and out on their own, however, his wife may now want to get a job out of the home, be more independent, and share more equally in the decision-making responsibilities with her husband. As he sees it, his wife's new attitude is a change in the relationship's contract. She has changed, and he has to change his values or he will find he will stop being in love with her. Going through such a transition period is often a difficult time for couples.

should we trust the feelings of love?

Trusting the feelings of love is an important area to explore briefly. When people are in love, they often let their feelings for their loved one dictate their behavior rather than relying on rational judgment. People who are in a state of Mature Love are less likely to do so, since they tend to rely not only on how they feel but also on what they think. As a result, their judgment is usually fairly sound. Romantic Love, though, is a different story. When individuals are in the throes of Romantic Love, they almost always let their feelings of love govern their behavior. As a result, their judgment is notoriously bad. Some psychologists refer to Romantic Love as neurotic love because people exercise such poor judgment and reasoning during the Romantic Love phase. As a general rule, you should never make a major decision about your life when in a state of Romantic Love. For example, you shouldn't get married, get a divorce, leave your spouse for the person you are having an affair with, or make any significant financial changes (i.e., give the new person you love a lot of money). In short, you shouldn't make any major changes in your life while in the state of Romantic Love. Such decisions are usually regretted later.

I once had a client who had been married thirty years and had two grown children. He had a brief affair, which he thought was true love. He was willing to leave his wife, whom he sincerely loved, for a divorced woman half his age who had three small children of her own. In addition, she was deeply in debt. He insisted to me that he would be happy with her entire family and all their problems. He could not be talked out of this conviction. I asked only that he wait several months before making this decision and leaving his wife. He waited a few months. Later, he told me he couldn't believe he had almost made "the biggest mistake in my life." People can do foolish things in the grip of Romantic Love. It is important not to act on your feelings when in the state of Romantic Love. On the other hand, when you are in Mature Love, your feelings can be a guide to understanding yourself and your loved one better. Your Mature Love feelings can usually be trusted as fairly accurate indicators of what is going on inside you. As such, your feelings can help you be closer to your spouse and aid you in making sound, rational decisions.

the difference between romantic love and mature love

We have looked at both Romantic Love and Mature Love. We have seen that while individuals are in Romantic Love it can be dangerous for them to rely only on their feelings when making decisions. But with Mature Love, trusting your feelings poses no great problem. Romantic and Mature Love are different in other ways as well. It may help to understand them better by comparing and contrasting them.

A first and obvious area of difference is in the nature of feelings. A major, if not the primary, ingredient of Romantic Love is a very powerful positive feeling and attraction for another person. Romantic Love is thus a euphoric "high." That kind of "high" does not characterize Mature Love, which is marked by a broader range of feelings, both positive and negative. The positive feelings are less frequently the "high" of Romantic Love but more often the feelings of caring, concern, and appreciation. Couples in Mature Love also experience negative feelings towards each other, such as anger, resentment, or disappointment. This broader range of feelings leads to a more complex type of interaction and, in the long run, to a deeper and more meaningful relationship. The attraction for loved ones in Romantic Love is almost exclusively sexual and romantic, while in Mature Love this intense attraction is lessened and, in its place, there is an appreciation for the spouse as a friend and as a person, as well as romantic and sexual feelings.

Time is something else that distinguishes Romantic from Mature Love. Romantic Love is time-limited. After three to six months, the intense feelings and attraction to one another start to wane, followed by a stage of Disappointment and Disillusionment. Mature Love, on the other hand, is not time-limited. It can last as long as the individuals involved grow as persons and as long as the relationship grows and develops.

A third characteristic that distinguishes Romantic Love from Mature Love is how people perceive those they love. In Romantic Love they perceive their loved ones in unrealistic, usually idealistic terms. A person in Romantic Love sees only the best of the other person. Perception gets distorted and most people see only that which they want to see, usually the perfect person of their dreams. In Mature Love, loved ones are viewed more realistically and perceived as they really are, with their faults and shortcomings as well as their strengths and positive attributes. Mature Love lets us see a three-dimensional person, whereas Romantic Love's view is one-dimensional.

12

The fourth characteristic that separates Mature Love from Romantic Love is the amount of time, work and commitment that it takes to make a love relationship successful. The major issues couples have to deal with are achieving sexual compatibility, becoming friends, solving differences, and being intimate with one another. In Romantic Love there is virtually no work involved as far as these issues are concerned. Everything comes easy or is free. In Romantic Love, sex is a delight, new and exciting. Couples are close as friends, even if they have nothing in common and rarely talk. In Romantic Love there are very few fights or squabbles, and couples make up quickly, though superficially. No real differences emerge during this time to require a couple to really grapple with conflicts or major disagreements between them. Neither do they need to work at achieving intimacy. Infatuation substitutes for intimacy and couples believe they are closer and more intimate than they really are. In short, Romantic Love really requires no hard work, which may be one reason it is so much fun and so enjoyable.

On the other hand, Mature Love requires hard work, time, and commitment. The issues of sexual compatibility, friendship, and solving problems require patience, perseverance, and lots of communication between people to be resolved successfully. Mature Love is not free or particularly easy; it's actually lots of work. For example, sexual compatibility is new during Romantic Love, when there is a high level of physical attraction. As a result, there is not much work necessary to maintain a successful sexual relationship. In Mature Love, the development of sexual compatibility requires lots of talking to one another, getting to know one another, and sharing on a more vulnerable and intimate basis. In addition, other areas of the relationship need to be running smoothly if there is to be an enjoyable sex relationship. Couples can't have unresolved conflicts and differences and still have a super sex life. Couples in Mature Love can enjoy a wonderful sexual relationship, but it requires personal commitment, and the investment of time and energy in one another. The rewards from Mature Love, then, are sizeable but not without a price. That price is hard work. In coming chapters we'll explore in detail what this work involves.

can the feelings of love be sustained over time?

If the enjoyable feelings of Romantic Love last only three to six months and then dissipate forever, the notion of Mature Love in some ways can appear pretty boring. Can the feelings and attraction that are experienced so strongly in Romantic Love be carried on, in some capacity, over time? My answer is a qualified yes, if certain criteria are met. In the next five chapters of this book we will cover these areas: effective interpersonal communication skills; developing sexual compatibility; finding ways to resolve conflict successfully; becoming emotionally intimate; and learning how to have fun and play together. I believe that, if a couple can deal with each of these areas to their mutual satisfaction, they can in great measure rejuvenate the feelings of Romantic Love and maintain a positive attraction for one another. If, on the other hand, breakdowns occur in any of these five areas, it will be difficult to maintain the feeling of love, and the relationship can become strained and problem-oriented. This book will explore the pitfalls of such self-defeating relationships and focus on how to treat them. And so, while they may not be as intense or as frequent as during the initial phase of Romantic Love, I firmly believe that romantic feelings *can* last a lifetime, if couples are willing to work hard to achieve certain objectives and goals. The rest of this book will tell you how.

2

necessary interpersonal skills: giving and assertion

So far, we have examined Romantic Love, why people fall in love with one person as opposed to another and the concept of Mature Love. Now we're going to begin to examine the steps needed to make a love relationship work. In this chapter we'll explore two important interpersonal skills that when used effectively provide an equitable balance to a relationship so that people can meet both their own and their loved ones' needs. These two skills are the ability to GIVE to your mate and the ability to be ASSERTIVE and stand up for yourself when dealing with your loved one.

Giving means meeting the needs of your partner by doing something pleasing and important to demonstrate your love. Your gift can be tangible — flowers, a night out, a special dinner — or it can be less tangible, such as the giving of your time and attention, or your willingness to listen to a problem.

Being *Assertive* refers to your being able to stand up for your own rights and needs. Assertion in this context refers to being able to stand up honestly to your loved one, to not allow him or her to take advantage of you, and to make sure that you are going to get your wants and needs met. For instance, you might express your preference for a movie that your partner might not enjoy. Or you might make clear your annoyance when your mate has been consistently late for dinner.

Both are skills which must be acquired before a successful male-female relationship can be established. Problems inevitably develop when these

15

skills are lacking. Both partners need to be able both to Give and to be Assertive. Anything short of this and the relationship will be in difficulty.

giving and listening

Giving refers to being able to meet the needs of your loved one. But it is
hard to give if you don't know the needs of your partner. If you can learn to listen and really understand, you will be able to learn what your partner regards
as important or wants and desires at a given moment. Giving sounds simple
and it would be relatively easy to give (unless you were flat broke) if most
needs were material in nature (i.e., flowers, a book, dinner out). Most giving,
however, consists of such intangibles as a bit of your time, a hug when you're
feeling lonely, five minutes to hear a problem, a smile and a kiss at the right
moment. These gifts are emotional in nature. Since they are less concrete,
they often get overlooked and ignored, especially when individuals get caught
up in the hectic process of day-to-day living.

To become an effective giver means learning how to listen. Listening is
both a skill and an art. *Listening simply means attempting to see the world
through another person's eyes*. You can understand other people only by listening to what they say and observing their body language and their actions.
To be a good listener means you don't talk, you don't interject your ideas, you
don't at this point share too much of yourself. Rather, you devote your full
attention to your spouse. You say to yourself, "How would I feel if I were in
Susan's shoes?" or "How do I think John feels and perceives things right
now?" When you listen you really get the opportunity to know your loved one.
A later chapter will show that listening can be very therapeutic and that it aids
in the process of solving personal problems, thus bringing couples closer together. But for now, learning to be a good listener will help your ability to give.
Good listening, then, sets the stage for good giving.

One reason listening is important is because many people find it difficult
to tell their loved ones what they need. It would help to be always assertive and
be able to say: "I need help with the kids. Please stay home and don't go bowling tonight." But too often people don't speak up; they only hope their partners
will know what they want and will somehow magically respond. As we'll see
shortly, it's your responsibility to be Assertive or you won't often get your
needs met. It also help to be a good listener, however, so that you can pick up
the hints and clues your mate gives you and thus understand what is
wanted.

The secret of understanding Giving as a concept is realizing that it
involves doing something special for your loved one because you know it's
something he or she wants or needs at that particular time. It is truly a gift. For

example, a husband listens to his wife's complaints about his long hours at work and his being away from the family from morning 'til late at night. As he listens, he realizes that his wife needs more closeness and intimacy from him than she has been receiving lately. He also knows that his own career is important and that he enjoys his work immensely. He's aware, however, that his wife's concerns are legitimate and important too. He decides to spend more time with his wife and family. It means readjusting his schedule, but he believes giving to his wife is important enough to make the effort. They decide to spend some evenings alone, away from the children, talking and dining out, something they have not done in quite a while.

We can see from this illustration how listening and Giving go hand in hand. It's hard to give something to your partner if you haven't first listened and found out what it is he or she needs. Giving brings people closer together.

A useful exercise in this regard is to spend some time listening to your mate. Really find out what your partner wants and needs; then practice Giving. Giving is a habit; the more you do it, the easier and more natural it feels. Also, the more you give, the more sensitive you become to what your partner wants from you.

assertiveness

Assertiveness means standing up for yourself and for your own rights and needs in the relationship. When you give, you want to do something for your partner. When you're Assertive, you want to do something for yourself. There are two major components to assertiveness. One area of assertiveness is standing up for your own rights. When you do this, you might be expressing your preference for a movie, where you want to go on vacation, or how you think the children should be disciplined. You are asserting your preferences, choices and values with the hope of convincing your partner to go along with you.

The other area of assertion deals with handling unacceptable behavior. In every human relationship, inevitably there are times when a person's behavior is going to be annoying and frustrating to his or her mate. If your partner's behavior is unacceptable, it interferes with your ability to meet your needs. For example, unacceptable behavior might be your partner's constantly interrupting you while you're trying to speak, never letting you finish a sentence. Or, your partner promises to pick you up after work and then shows up half an hour late while you've been waiting, soaking wet, in the rain. Or your partner breaks a precious possession through carelessness. It will always be true that partners in a relationship will do things that frustrate and annoy each other. What is important is how you choose to respond to your loved one's behavior. Here Assertion, or confrontation, is defined as dealing with your negative feelings (usually anger) toward your mate.

Being Assertive, then, deals with two areas: standing up for yourself by expressing your preferences and desires, and dealing with your partner's unacceptable behavior.

You can choose to confront your mate and to take care of your own needs in three different ways: by being passive, assertive, or aggressive. Of these three, being assertive is the most appropriate and useful way to get your needs met while still respecting the rights of your loved one. The other two approaches are not usually helpful in meeting your own needs, and they are also disruptive to a harmonious relationship.

If your are upset with your partner and choose to be passive (i.e., say little or nothing about what is bothering you), your mate doesn't know how you feel. Passivity can be expressed in several ways, such as being silent, hinting at displeasure, or pouting. None of these methods directly tells your partner how you feel, and you often leave your mate guessing about what you mean. Your needs are unknown because you haven't voiced them. The consequence of being passive is that your needs are not met because you haven't been direct and open about how you feel. As time goes on, your partner, unable to read your mind and thus meet your needs, will take advantage of you. You will then feel a good deal of resentment which will in turn jeopardize the relationship.

If, on the other hand, you're aggressive instead of passive, you attempt to get your needs met but in a manner which personally attacks your mate. Aggressive responses are often expressed by blaming, demanding, criticizing or yelling.

When you are aggressive, your loved one usually responds in one of two ways: withdrawing and giving in (a passive response), at the same time feeling a good deal of anger and resentment; or becoming aggressive and fighting back in a similar manner. When you are aggressive you may get your way, but it will be at the expense of not meeting your loved one's needs. In the long run, being consistently aggressive is very damaging to a relationship.

The best way to meet your own needs and keep a good relationship is to be Assertive. Assertiveness means that you are honest and open with your negative feelings and that you express your wants and desires. You tell your mate how you really feel. You don't hide your anger and hold it in (as in being passive). On the other hand, you don't attack and belittle your loved one (as in being aggressive). Rather, you deal with your feelings and your needs in a direct and genuine way.

18

The goal is twofold: to meet your needs without sacrificing your partner's needs. The result is a better relationship in the long run, with a good chance of modifying your loved one's behavior into something more acceptable. Given the three styles of behavior, it is easy to conclude that being Assertive is the most effective method of modifying people's behavior while meeting your needs and maintaining positive relationships with them.

giving and assertion

To enter into a male-female relationship and make it successful, everyone needs to possess these two interpersonal skills: first, the ability to Give and the ability to be sensitive to and meet the needs of another. Without both abilities, a relationship cannot grow and flourish, since no one wants to feel emotionally uncared for. Second, everyone needs to be able to be Assertive and stand up for oneself, even to a loved one. You have to represent yourself. You can't expect the person you love to read your mind and intuitively sense your needs. It is your responsibility to meet your needs in an assertive — not a passive or aggressive — manner. What is critical in the area of interpersonal skills, then, is that you are able not only to give but to stand up to the one you love, thereby meeting the needs of both of you.

having only one skill

The importance of having both these interpersonal skills cannot be stressed enough. From my own clinical experience working with couples, I have learned that if each person hasn't acquired these skills, the relationship is in for trouble. Very often when a couple comes in for counseling, each person turns out to be good at just *one* skill. For example, a wife may be excellent at Giving, but she has great difficulty standing up to her husband and being Assertive in getting her own needs met. The husband in this marriage is Assertive and stands up for himself by asking, demanding, and expecting things from his wife, but is very negligent at Giving to her. In such a case, the wife becomes the giver and the husband becomes the taker. This arrangement leads to a very lopsided and ultimately unsatisfactory relationship for both people. From my experience with couples who have this problem, I find that most often the woman is the giver and the man is the taker. Despite women's liberation, women are still culturally trained to give and not to be assertive. For men the opposite is true.

giving but nonassertive

Look at what happens when couples have only one of the two necessary skills. Take the example of the Giving but nonassertive wife, and the problems her imbalance in skills creates for her. The wife is dissatisfied because she's not getting many of her needs met. She gives to her husband but he doesn't return the favor. She is confused and perplexed. She feels unloved because her husband doesn't give to her, and she develops a growing resentment towards him. Why doesn't he give to her?

A giving but nonassertive person almost always believes that "Giving begets giving." This is not true. The truth is, giving begets *taking*. If you constantly give to someone without letting your needs be known (i.e., you are passive), you and your giving will be taken for granted. Under such circumstances, an Assertive partner often becomes an aggressive one, expecting and demanding everything, and of course failing to meet the needs of the passive partner. So giving by itself does not beget giving. You need to learn to be Assertive to get your mate to give to you. I have confronted women who were just givers and said, "If you want your man to give to you, it's going to take more than just your giving to him. You are also going to have to stand up and be assertive with him. You need to tell him what you want. If you are both giving and assertive, he will then give to you in return." But the response I get from such Giving, nonassertive woman usually goes something like this: "If I have to ask him for something I want, it's not the same thing; I want him to give to me spontaneously, from his own free choice." Or "If I have to ask him to give to me, how do I know he really wants to do it? Isn't he just doing it because I am making him do it?"

Both of these questions have to do with the intent behind the giving. Asking these questions shows that the woman's concern is not just the man's giving, but more importantly, that it be giving that comes from the heart. In fact, both men and women want giving to be motivated by love and a sincere desire to please. It may help you understand the issue of Giving better by distinguishing between two types of Giving: Giving based on need and Giving based on desire.

tit for tat giving

Giving because you need to give occurs when your partners says something like this: "Let's give tit for tat. I'll give to you and meet some of your needs and I'll expect you to give to me. Here are some of my needs." You thus give to your mate for two reasons: one, you now know what your partner's needs are; and two, the implication is clear that if you do not give, you are not going to receive. This is Tit for Tat Giving, and I believe it comes *before* the second kind of giving, Giving From the Heart.

giving from the heart

Giving From the Heart is motivated by a sense of altruism. Here you give not because you feel compelled to, but because you want to. You also give because you know your giving pleases your loved one.

It is this type of giving that the woman was referring to in the earlier example when she stated, "I want him to give from his own free choice and because he really wants to." The important point to understand is that Tit for Tat Giving is a necessary prerequisite to Giving From the Heart. Tit for Tat Giving must come first. Individuals give initially because their partners inform them of their needs and put on the pressure to have those needs met. Thus you give at first because you realize that your loved one expects it and that if you don't come through, your own needs won't be met. Once an effective pattern of Tit for Tat Giving is established, there is a mutual taking care of each other. As you get into the habit of giving, your giving comes more and more out of your love and concern for your mate, rather than from a feeling that you have to do it. Then you are truly Giving From the Heart.

If you are a person who gives easily but has difficulty being Assertive, you don't need to stop Giving. You do need to start being Assertive, however, in communicating your wants and needs. Your Assertion leads to receiving Tit for Tat Giving from your partner. As this type of giving is successful, it leads to Giving From the Heart. The nature of giving will change however, if you give freely but are not Assertive, for what starts out for you as Giving From the Heart turns into Giving Out of Obligation if not reciprocated. Here you resent Giving but do so anyway from a sense of duty. This type of Giving almost always results when you have *not* been Assertive about your needs and/or your partner does not reciprocate your giving. Over time, Giving Out of Obligation seriously harms a relationship. The best antidote is learning to be Assertive so you increase the likelihood of getting your own needs met. As you get your needs met, you will give more from desire rather than duty.

assertive but not giving

What about the person who is Assertive but does not Give much? Can this person change and become more loving and Giving? As we noted earlier, the Assertive nongiving partner is generally — but not always — the man. Before looking at the problem of learning to be more Giving, let's explore some of the reasons why people don't Give.

The main reason the Assertive nongiving person does not Give is because the mate doesn't request or, if necessary, demand it. A typical couple with this problem is one in which the man expects the woman to meet many of his needs and she initially does Give freely and openly to him. Since she puts no overt pressure on him to meet her needs, he gives little in return. Over time her genuine Giving either becomes Giving Out of Obligation or she stops Giving at all, if her needs are not met. The result, of course, is disaster for the relationship. When the woman stops Giving but remains passive, it is likely that the man will not only be Assertive but become aggressive when his needs are not met. Such a situation can lead to open argument or silent warfare, with each person withdrawing from the other. A further complication is that Assertive, at times aggressive, nongiving partners tend to lose respect for their more passive mates, simply because their mates are nonassertive. With loss of respect, love diminishes and so does the desire to Give, especially Giving From the Heart.

How, then, does one get a nongiving partner to be more Giving and loving emotionally? The best method is to be more Assertive yourself, stating clearly what you want and need. In addition to being Assertive, you need to make your own Giving contingent upon getting from your loved one. In essence, you say you are willing to Give but you want your needs met too or you'll stop Giving. Such a statement sounds harsh but it's the best way to get a nongiving mate to start Giving. Lectures and logical arguments don't work here. This approach is the Tit for Tat Giving previously discussed. Nongiving partners, then, are being taught to give by having pressure put on them. Their giving is not yet Giving From the Heart. Remember, as nongiving mates learn to give Tit for Tat, they then develop the ability to Give From the Heart. So, they need to be taught by Assertive mates to give Tit for Tat, and over a period of time they will also learn to Give From the Heart.

How important is it, then, for a couple to have both sets of skills, skills to insure that the needs of both partners will be met? When each partner possesses both Giving and Assertive skills, they are ready to form a balanced and *equal* love relationship. Without these skills, relationships quickly become lopsided, with one and usually both people frustrated and unhappy.

summary

We have seen in this chapter that if you can develop two important inter-personal skills — learning to Give and being Assertive — you are going to have a relationship that is balanced, in which both partners are treated as equals. This balance leads to both self-respect and respect for your loved one. Self-respect generates increased self-esteem. Respect for your loved one generates greater feelings of love. These skills are also negotiation skills in that they set the stage for developing sexual harmony, resolving conflict and in deciding how to spend mutually enjoyable time together, topics we'll address in the following chapters of this book.

3

*achieving sexual compatibility**

Feelings of love often act as the glue that holds the relationship together during stormy and difficult times. The interpersonal skills of Giving and Assertion insure a balanced, equitable relationship. Without both these things, couples can begin to drift apart.

A satisfying sexual relationship, like the feelings of love and the skills of Giving and Assertion, brings personal pleasure and enjoyment and also strengthens and enriches a relationship. Sexual responsiveness for both men and women can be very fragile. In this chapter you will learn what can be done to maintain and enhance a good sexual relationship.

sexual acceptance and personal-emotional acceptance

Men and women have two fundamental needs that must be met if couples are to have a rewarding sexual relationship. These needs are for sexual acceptance and personal-emotional acceptance. *Sexual Acceptance* refers to being accepted and valued as a sexual being. Individuals feel sexually accepted when they feel their mates are sexually attracted to them and are responsive to their sexual overtures. This attraction is expressed in such indirect sexual play as kidding, teasing and flirting. It is also expressed in more direct sexual ways, such as kissing, foreplay, and sexual intercourse. The main element of Sexual Acceptance is your feeling you are unique and special in a sexual sense to your loved one.

You feeling that your are sexually accepted by your partner is one of the major things that makes you feel that you are loved by your mate. As a result

---

* I am greatly indebted to Mike and Joyce Grace, *A Joyful Meeting: Sexuality and Marriage*, for the ideas on which this chapter is based.

25

of Sexual Acceptance, you not only feel a greater attraction to your loved one but you feel better about yourself as a person.

With Sexual Acceptance you feel valued as a sexual being. *Personal-Emotional Acceptance* refers to being valued as a person in your own right. Personal-Emotional Acceptance is the feeling that your mate loves you for who you are. You feel appreciated, cared about, valued as a human being. You sense that your partner is willing to take the time and make the effort to meet your personal needs and desires, whether by bringing you a gift, going out to dinner, or just sitting and talking to you. When you feel Personal Acceptance, as when you feel Sexual Acceptance, you feel loved. Men and women both have the need for Sexual and Personal-Emotional Acceptance.

the priority of sexual and personal-emotional acceptance

A couple achieves sexual compatibility in a relationship when both the man and the woman are able to meet these two needs of Sexual and Personal-Emotional Acceptance. Everyone has both needs, but a basic problem couples face is that men and women have a different priority for these needs.

Let's look at this in detail. Traditionally most often men's primary need is for Sexual Acceptance from the female. Women, on the other hand, regard Personal-Emotional Acceptance from the male as the number one priority. As each gets the primary need fulfilled, the other basic need becomes important. That is, the man now wants Personal-Emotional Acceptance and the woman now wants Sexual Acceptance. The following diagram illustrates this principle:

DIAGRAM I

Typical Priority of Needs for Men and Women		
	Male	*Female*
Primary Need	Sexual Acceptance	Personal-Emotional Acceptance
Secondary Need	Personal-Emotional Acceptance	Sexual Acceptance

This is a broadly-stated general rule, and the priorites can be reversed with some men and women, but in the majority of cases I've dealt with, it holds true.

This picture is further complicated by the fact that both individuals need to get their primary need met as a *prerequisite* to feeling loved. Thus, for a man to feel loved by a woman he must feel that she accepts him sexually. If he does not feel that she accepts him sexually (i.e., that she is sexually responsive and accepting of his overtures), he quite often does not feel he is truly loved. The same is true for the woman regarding her primary need. She must receive Personal-Emotional Acceptance from the male (i.e., she must feel cared about, appreciated, and valued for the person she is) before she feels she is loved. The following diagram presents this phenomenon graphically:

DIAGRAM II

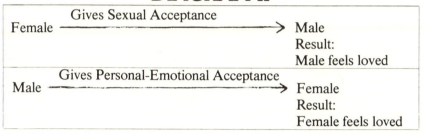

Thus, both men and women require that their separate primary needs be met before they feel their mate loves them. *A further complication to this picture is that each wants to have his or her own primary need met before meeting the other's primary need.* The implications of this notion are somewhat staggering. It means, for example, that men want to be sexually accepted before they want to — or perhaps are even able to — be responsive on a personal-emotional level. Women want to be accepted personally-emotionally and appreciated before they respond to the man on a sexual level. The result is a very delicate but interdependent relationship between men and women, which can be diagrammed as follows:

27

DIAGRAM III

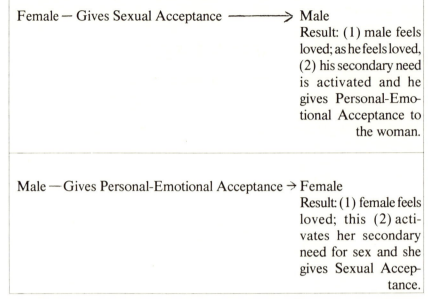

Female — Gives Sexual Acceptance ⟶ Male

Result: (1) male feels loved; as he feels loved, (2) his secondary need is activated and he gives Personal-Emotional Acceptance to the woman.

Male — Gives Personal-Emotional Acceptance → Female

Result: (1) female feels loved; this (2) activates her secondary need for sex and she gives Sexual Acceptance.

We thus see that men want Sexual Acceptance first. Once they feel sexually appreciated and cared for, their secondary need for Personal-Emotional Acceptance is activated. The man can then respond to a woman at a personal level which meets her primary need to be valued and cared for as a unique human being. After this occurs, a woman's secondary need for sexual responsivity is activated and she can respond to the man on a sexual level. The result is each meets the other's primary need; in doing so each sets the stage to get his or her own needs met.

To summarize: for a positive sexual relationship to develop, the following must occur. Either the man or the woman gives to the other. It doesn't matter who goes first. For example, if the woman is sexually responsive to the man, the man feels loved by the woman and in turn he feels love for her. As he feels loving feelings towards her he is not only sexually responsive to her but, more importantly for her needs, he gives Personal-Emotional Acceptance to her, meeting her primary need. Namely, he is tender, caring and appreciative of her individual wants and desires. (We must remember the male's primary need for sexual acceptance has to be met before he gives at the personal-emotional level.) He now both wants to respond to the woman on a personal level and is receptive to her responding to him on this level. The same is true of the woman. When she feels cared about and appreciated as a person, she finds that she now feels sexually aroused and is interested in responding to her mate in a sexual manner. As each responds to the other's needs, a positive cycle is established. Now the man and the woman are meeting *both* of their needs. Each feels sexually responsive to the other and cared about as a person. The

28

result is a sexually satisfying relationship. The following diagram illustrates this scenario:

DIAGRAM IV

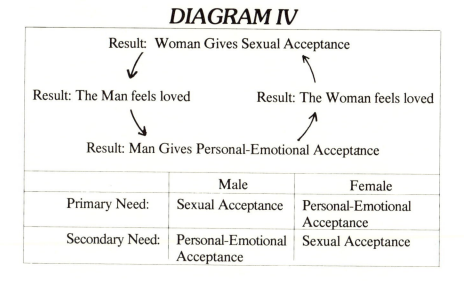

	Male	Female
Primary Need:	Sexual Acceptance	Personal-Emotional Acceptance
Secondary Need:	Personal-Emotional Acceptance	Sexual Acceptance

understanding the priority of needs

Although this chapter stresses that men and women often give these basic needs different priorities, wide variations from the model I've described above can and do exist, and are perfectly normal. I have treated couples whose needs were reversed, the male wanting Personal-Emotional Acceptance first and the woman having Sexual Acceptance as her number one priority. I have also seen a few couples whose needs were identical in order of priority. Finally, with advancing age, many males find their need for Personal-Emotional Acceptance becoming as important, if not more important than, Sexual Acceptance. Keep in mind that normal variations from the model that is being presented here do occur when analyzing your own sexual attitudes and those of your loved one. Remember, the order or the priority of your needs, no matter what is it, is normal and acceptable.

sexual compatibility — a case illustration

Let's take a concrete example to illustrate this process. Jim and Carol have been married for about one year. When they first met they were immediately attracted to one another and became romantically involved. Both were sexually and emotionally attracted to one another. Carol expressed her sexual attraction openly and caringly. Men often feel that when the woman is sexually responsive she is allowing herself to be vulnerable. As a man perceives the woman as vulnerable, he feels he too can be vulnerable. Men often manifest their vulnerability by being more open themselves, sharing their personal feelings, and disclosing themselves at a deeper level. As Jim felt Carol's sexual acceptance and responsiveness to him, he felt cared about and valued as someone important to her. As a result, he began to share more of himself as a person, as well as being attentive to her needs. He took time to listen to her, to give her flowers, and to do the special loving things she wanted. He responded to her in such a way that she felt prized for who she was and not simply as a sex object.

In short, Jim and Carol met the other's primary need. She valued him sexually; he valued her as a unique and special person in his life. As they responded in this manner, it activated or liberated their secondary needs. As Carol felt really cared about, valued and special to Jim as a person, she began to respond more sexually. Her sexual responsiveness now had more real meaning for her. Sex was important and significant in her life, and she now became more sexually responsive to Jim at a deeper level than before. Feeling that Carol cared about him sexually and romantically, Jim felt freer in sharing and being more fully himself in the relationship. He trusted his personal feelings more and shared them openly. In addition, he took more time and attention to meet and fulfill Carol's personal-emotional needs. As Jim felt sexually accepted he became sensitive to his own needs for Personal-Emotional Acceptance. He realized he liked being more open himself, and that he enjoyed the emotional closeness the relationship provided. He also enjoyed giving to Carol and seeing her appreciate his gifts. As both Jim's and Carol's primary needs were met, their secondary needs came into prominence and became just as significant and important as their primary needs.

We see, then, that with Jim and Carol a positive cycle was created. Almost simultaneously, she responds to him sexually and he to her on a personal-emotional basis. As these responses occur, each feels caring and cared for. They say to themselves: "You are showing me you love me because you are attempting to meet my needs." Then each attempts to fulfill the other's needs and in the process they begin to meet their own secondary needs. The woman gets in touch more with her own sexuality and sexual responsiveness, and the man begins to fulfill his emotional needs more. In this relationship, both people are happy and fulfilled. We have a positive cycle that becomes self-reinforcing.

how couples
can become sexually incompatible

A sexual relationship seems often to be very positive, like the one we just described, or very negative. Usually it works well or not at all, and there's not much in-between. The reason for this all-or-nothing phenomenon is that when there is a breakdown in the sexual relationship, it seems quite complete. Let's examine why. As we have seen, the fact that men's and women's needs with respect to being sexually responsive have different priorities, creates a rather delicate balance which when maintained works very well. When this balance is disrupted for some reason, however, everything usually comes to a grinding halt. For example, if the man stops being caring and concerned, if he stops doing the little things that show the woman he appreciates her, over time she will believe her mate doesn't care for her anymore. The result is she will not feel loved. *Because she no longer feels loved and appreciated she will turn off sexually*. Because she is not responsive to his sexual overtures, the male no longer feels loved and valued. *The man feels hurt and angry. As a consequence, he stops giving on the personal-emotional level.*

As this occurs, both now put pressure on their partner to meet their separate primary needs. The man puts pressure on the woman for sex, requesting and at times demanding sexual attention. This behavior turns her off sexually even more. The woman in turn puts pressure on the man to care more about her and her needs as a person. Each feels the other is demanding without giving in return. The result is bitterness, hurt, anger — and problems in their sexual relationship.

why we have affairs

When there is a breakdown in the sexual relationship, people at times turn to others and have affairs. Men and women often have affairs for different reasons, however. Women have affairs to feel cared about, to be treated as special and important, to be appreciated as a person. Sex is not so important to them. On the other hand, men usually have affairs for sexual acceptance. They want a woman to like them for their good looks, to see them as sexy as well as sexually satisfying. Men and women then have affairs to fulfill the primary need that they feel their partner is not meeting.

31

a breakdown in sexual compatibility
— a case illustration

Now we need to look at a case example that illustrates how a negative self-reinforcing cycle can develop and harm a couple's sexual relationship. Dean and Sara have been married for twenty years and have two teenage sons. Though they have had some ups and downs in their marriage, by and large their relationship could be described in positive terms. According to Sara, their biggest problem (which began a year ago, after Dean received a job promotion), is that Dean is too preoccupied with his career and leaves too much of the housework, bills, and disciplining of the children to her. Much of the time Sara does not feel special or important to Dean. She says, "He pays attention to me when he wants sex." At other times "he ignores me," and is either working on his job or out playing ball with the boys.

For Dean, sports have always been important. He played college baseball and is now helping his two teenage sons (both on the school baseball team) with practice sessions every day. He feels he needs to spend time with his sons because in a few years they will be off to college and on their own. These high school years are his last chance to spend some quality time with them, he reasons. Dean also feels that, since he works hard to provide for his family, his wife has to assume more of the household chores and responsibilities. Though this has been the pattern of their marriage for many years, Dean's new promotion a year ago, and his resulting additional commitment to his job, have left little special time for him and Sara.

Shortly after Dean's job promotion, he and Sara began to experience sexual difficulty. Dean worked hard and was often tired at night. He didn't attempt to meet Sara's needs for Personal-Emotional Acceptance; often he just wanted to have sex and go to sleep. Under this arrangement Sara began to feel used. She felt Dean didn't really want to be with her and enjoy her company, but that he was just "horny" and she was convenient. Dean felt Sara was not sexually attracted to him and was intentionally "withholding." As a result, they both felt frustrated and angry.

More and more frequently Dean's needs for Sexual Acceptance were not met; neither were Sara's needs for Personal-Emotional Acceptance. Because of their hurt and anger, both Dean and Sara wittingly or unwittingly stopped meeting each other's primary need. Each began putting pressure on the other to meet his or her own needs while, at the same time, abandoning any sincere attempt to meet the other's needs.

The result for Dean and Sara is typical of many couples who have this problem. Dean feels Sara never wants to have sex and is intentionally withholding sex from him. "What's wrong with her?" he demands. "Do we have to go out, do I always have to buy her dinner, get her flowers before we can jump in the sack? Can't we just make love and enjoy ourselves without all the preliminaries each time?'' Dean thinks sex should have the same meaning for Sara as it does for him as a male. When Sara doesn't respond sexually, he feels hurt, angry and then unloved. As a result, he tends to withhold from Sara the emotional support and affection that would, in the long run, help him get his own needs met.

As Sara feels unloved she says, "Dean just wants sex. He's not interested in me. I can't just jump up and have sex at his beck and call. It's not meaningful for me that way. Dean can be in the middle of something and he wants to stop and have sex out of the clear blue. I want to get things done and accomplished first and then feel we are close before we have sex." Here Sara expresses the sentiment many women have that she wants her needs for Personal-Emotional Acceptance met first before she can become sexually responsive. In this case, since neither partner was meeting the other's primary need, both stopped giving and each felt hurt, resentful, and unloved. As might be expected, their sex life suffered greatly. They often went months without sex and rarely felt close to one another. This is an unfortunate but often common pattern for couples when they don't understand and resolve their differences in the area of their sexual relationship.

the security-protection need

We have stated throughout this chapter that the needs for Sexual Acceptance and Personal-Emotional Acceptance are two basic needs of men and women, needs that have to be acknowledged if we are to understand how to achieve sexual compatibility in an on-going love relationship. Now we want to discuss a third need that is also present and becomes more pronounced when a couple has children. It is the need for security and protection. The Security-Protection Need refers to the desire to be provided for emotionally and at times also financially.

This need is much stronger and more evidenced in women than men, especially when a couple has young children. A woman at this time needs to feel that she, as a mother, and the children are being taken care of and provided for by the man. The feeling of family is very important to the woman. In fact, this need predominates over her other needs for Personal-Emotional Acceptance and Sexual Acceptance during this time. As a result, the husband who wants his wife to be sexually responsive must first provide for her Security-Protection needs and her needs for Personal-Emotional Acceptance before she will be sexually responsive to him. If they don't feel their other two needs are being met, women often don't feel very sexual. It should

33

also be remembered however, that men also have this need for security and protection and it usually manifests itself in their fear of being replaced or left by the woman. Men want a sense of security in the relationship and a sense of feeling part of a family just as the woman does.

Let's illustrate the importance of this Security-Protection Need with the case of Randy and Sue. They have been married seven years and have two small children, ages five and two. Randy is a guidance counselor; Sue works part-time doing secretarial work and babysitting. A year and a half ago, Randy decided to take a six-month leave of absence from his job to finish a master's thesis and also to do some major home repair work. This leave of absence was going to create some economic hardship for the family and Sue felt uneasy about this, with two small children to feed. But Randy assured her he would be able to get a better paying job as a result of completing his graduate work and so Sue reluctantly acquiesced to the plan.

Randy procrastinated over most of the six months, however, failing to finish his studies and not doing any of the needed home repair work. Sue was shocked and hurt by Randy's behavior at first. Over time she developed a growing resentment towards her husband. Sue felt let down by Randy; her sense of security and need for protection and support, with two small children, were endangered. She worried now how they would survive economically. She took two part-time jobs. After Randy's six-month leave was up, he returned to his old job. Once he was working again, they had enough money and became financially stable once more, but the damage had been done. Sue had lost faith in Randy as a provider. Randy had violated Sue's need for security-protection. In her mind Randy had not taken care of the family as he had promised. Needless to say, not only did their sexual frequency decrease during the six months of Randy's leave, but over a year later their sex life was still suffering greatly. Sue was just not interested in sex; a more basic need of hers was not being fulfilled. We see then the importance of understanding sexual responsiveness in the context of other needs. Once again, it is apparent that men and women differ in the priority they give sex in their lives.

personal problems and sexual responsiveness

One last thing often seems to separate men and women in the area of sex, and that is the role that problems play in their lives. As a general rule, when they have a problem such as studying for an exam, feeling overworked on their job, having loads of housework, or struggling with some personal matter, women don't normally enjoy taking a break to make love. Usually they want to finish whatever it is they are working on first. After it's done they are more

34

sexually responsive. Men are often just the opposite when it comes to dealing with a problem and their sexual responsiveness. A man can be wrestling with a problem (i.e., feeling frustrated over paying the bills or figuring up the income tax) and in the middle of it all jump up and say, "Honey, let's take a break and go jump in the sack." Men don't normally need to complete a task or resolve a problem before they are interested in sex. This difference can be a sore point for couples if they don't understand each other's attitude. Take the following example:

Ralph and Peggy were first-year law students and kept very busy with work and school schedules. Both worked exceptionally hard but when it came to sex each responded differently under the pressures of law school. Ralph got frustrated with his work and at times just wanted to set it all aside and make love. Peggy was forever putting him off, saying, "Let me get this paper done (or this report written)." Conflicts arose until they learned that each responded differently to pressures and problems when it came to making love. Peggy wanted to get things resolved, completed, before she made love. Ralph wanted to escape his frustrations and take a break to make love. Learning to appreciate and accept their differences in this area helped them to find satisfactory solutions with respect to their lovemaking.

As we see, men and women are different when it comes to how and under what conditions they are sexually responsive. For men, women can seem very frustrating. Women want their Security-Protection Needs met, their Personal-Emotional Needs met, and then to have no problems, nothing else occupying their minds, before they are sexually responsive. Women are also often frustrated by men, seeing them as wanting only sex and not being interested in other aspects of their relationship. Finding sexual compatibility seems like a big bill to fill. Let's see what steps can be taken to develop a more harmonious sexual relationship.

what can be done?

The question arises: if men and women are usually this different in the area of their sexuality, how can they develop some form of sexual compatibility? There are three basic things a couple can do that will increase the likelihood of their having a more satisfying sexual relationship.

First and foremost, there must be a recognition of differences: a man's basic need is for Sexual Acceptance, followed by Personal-Emotional Acceptance; a woman's basic need is first for Personal-Emotional Acceptance, along with a feeling of security and protection, followed finally by Sexual Acceptance. Men and women generally follow this pattern. Sometimes couples have the reverse pattern, with the man wanting Personal-Emotional

35

Acceptance first and the woman placing Sexual Acceptance as her number one priority. This pattern is also normal but doesn't occur as frequently. What is important for couples to understand is that each will usually have a different set of priorities in the area of sex.

Problems begin when couples don't understand and accept the fact that men and women differ in their attitudes towards sex. So many times men ask, "Why can't she just want sex for sex's sake and that's it?" Women say, "I want to be cared about, treated as a special person, and in that context sex is great." The first step, then, is to acknowledge that men and women are different and to accept that difference. Neither should try to change the other, but rather should simply accept each other as he or she is.

The second step in creating a harmonious and joyful sexual relationship is learning to put your loved one's needs before your own. You create conflict for yourself when you expect your partner to be just like you, and then refuse to budge unless your needs are met *first*. If a man recognizes that the woman needs to feel special, protected, and appreciated before she feels comfortable being sexual, it will be in his best interest to meet her needs first, rather than expecting her to be sexually responsive in the same way he is. If he builds a positive relationship by consistently fulfilling her needs to feel loved, she will respond to him on a sexual level much of the time. This method requires patience and the ability and willingness to place someone else's needs before your own.

The woman must also accept that men need sexual acceptance to feel loved. This does not mean, however, that a woman should have sex with her partner simply because he wants it. If she's not in the mood at all and is preoccupied with other things, she can't have sex without feeling resentment. This acceptance does mean, though, that a woman needs to respond to a man on a sexual level with flirting, joking, showing him he is important to her in a sexual way.

Both a man and a woman, then, need to accept not only that men and women are psychologically different when it comes to sex, but also that each must also work actively to meet the other's primary need to ensure that his or her own are met. If each works doubly hard to meet the other's need, the sex relationship will be successful.

A man, then, must provide a sense of protection and security for his partner. He must treat her as special and appreciate her as a person. He must also accept that there are times when matters such as financial problems or concerns about children are more important to her than sex. Likewise, the woman must realize the importance of sexual acceptance to the male and be responsive to his needs in this area.

The third and final thing couples can do to bring greater harmony and sexual compatibility to their relationship is to learn to communicate effectively with each other. Of all the areas in a relationship, sex and feelings about sex are often the most difficult to talk about. Couples are often willing to talk openly and listen to each other's points of view on religion, politics, money, or in-laws, but they find it far more difficult to discuss sex in honest, open terms. Far too often they become defensive, guarded or worse, silent, about how they feel about their sexual needs, desires, hopes, and fears. Many problems can be resolved when feelings are openly shared and couples listen effectively to one another. So, good communication skills, especially listening, giving, and being self-disclosing and assertive about needs, can be real assets in resolving problems and understanding each other better, which will help couples achieve sexual compatibility.

summary

Both the feelings of love (examined in a previous chapter) and sexual compatibility (as seen in this chapter) are very important to creating and maintaining a successful love relationship. But the feelings of love and sexual compatibility are very delicate issues that can work wonderfully or disastrously for us. We have noted that to achieve a sexually compatible relationship couples must understand that men and women are different in sexual responsiveness, that a loved one's needs must be put before your own, and that communication between couples must be honest and open.

A further key to understanding how to maintain a good sexual relationship is dealing with other areas of our relationship successfully. Specifically, in the next three chapters we will be dealing with resolving conflicts, being intimate, and having fun together.

All these issues are interrelated, even circular: success in one area makes it easier to be successful in another area. Sexual compatibility makes it easier to resolve conflicts and the ability to resolve conflicts helps make possible a more satisfactory sexual relationship.

4

couple conflict

introduction

An area of major importance to maintaining a successful love relationship is learning how to handle conflict constructively. In every close, loving relationship, there are going to be times when couples disagree with one another. Each gets under the other's skin. Women do things men don't like and men likewise annoy women. Such conflict is neither bad nor, for that matter, good; it is simply an inevitable facet of relationships. The important thing is not that couples have differences but *how* they resolve them. Thus, successful relationships are not defined by the number of arguments that arise, but rather by the methods that are employed to solve them. In this chapter, we will be exploring ways to settle differences in a healthy, democratic manner.

It is important to understand that you can fight or argue over almost anything imaginable. It can range from the proverbial squeezing of the toothpaste tube to whether you should have children, from how you should invest your money to which movie to see. The list of potential disagreements is endless. The basis of any fight or argument is a disagreement about how a problem should be solved. If you insist on doing something your own way, or your mate's behavior crosses over the line from what you consider acceptable to unacceptable, then you feel your needs are being infringed upon and you become frustrated, hurt or angry. When your mate refuses to do what you want and you refuse to change, the stage is set for conflict.

why couples fight

Why does it seem so easy to get into an argument with someone you love and care for so much? Some of the common reasons have to do with the fact that people fight with those to whom they are closest. You're far more willing to let your family see you as you really are than to expose your true self to an outsider. Furthermore, the tension and pressure people feel in their lives normally gets "dumped" on a loved one and family. The major reason people have arguments, however, is that everybody has learned to do things his or her own way; all the way from squeezing the toothpaste tube to analyzing the world situation. Doing things your personal way is a result of your growing-up experiences, the way in which your parents raised you and the manner in which your own personal style and values have evolved over time. Since each individual is different, each brings to a love relationship different ways of doing things.

For example, Sue came from a family that believed "cleanliness is next to godliness." Her parents' house was spotless. Sue had lived alone for four years after leaving home; her apartment, like her parents' home, was always immaculate. Bob, her boyfriend, came from a home environment where great emphasis was placed on academic and career achievement, with little attention devoted to maintaining a clean household. Bob, one of eight children, never remembered the house being clean or anyone much caring if the house was picked up. Conflicts arose shortly after Bob and Sue moved in with each other. Bob left his shoes, shorts and pants around the house, didn't pick up after himself, and had little interest in the house being "super-clean." Sue was angry with Bob's "sloppy household values," as she called them, and distressed at his lack of interest in keeping a clean, orderly house or in helping her with household chores. A clean house did not have the same value for Bob that it did for Sue. The result was many arguments over how clean the house should be and who should do the cleaning.

Couples must accept conflicts such as these as an inevitable part of life. The goal should always be to find ways of dealing with such conflicts successfully. If the resolution of the conflict is positive (i.e., both parties win), not only is a problem solved but the partners grow as individuals and their relationship is strengthened. Successful resolution of conflict also creates positive and beneficial effects in other areas of the relationship, such as sex and mutual feelings of love.

We are going to break down the remainder of this chapter into two parts. In the first part, we're going to look at four different methods of resolving an argument. The first two methods normally don't work, often creating more problems than they solve and impacting negatively on relationships. The last two methods result in a positive outcome and allow both parties to win. The second part of the chapter will be devoted to looking at the skills and steps couples need to have and to take to insure that conflicts have a positive rather than a negative outcome.

Part I/ two elements of a conflict

First, we need to understand that there are two basic elements to every conflict situation that arises between people, regardless of the nature of their relationship: husband and wife, parent and child, teacher and student, or boss and subordinate. The first element is the *actual problem* to be solved. Going back to the example of Bob and Sue, we recall that the problem to be solved was how clean the house should be kept and whose responsibility it was to keep it clean. The second element inherent in every conflict is the issue of *mutual relationship*. Mutual relationship refers to how couples feel about each other: do they have good or bad feelings toward one another? Do they feel finished with an argument, or are they still hurt, angry and bitter after a fight? For example, after an argument over household chores, Bob and Sue could feel angry and resentful or happy and content.

These two elements, the *problem* and the *relationship*, will come into play anytime an argument occurs. Each of these issues can have either a *positive* or *negative* influence. That is, the couple can either solve the problem or not, and they can have either good or bad feelings toward each other at the end of an argument. The different combinations of these two issues (problem and relationship) and the two different outcomes (positive or negative) lead to four types of conflict resolution. The four types are:

Number 1 BOTH LOSE
(Problem: Not Solved.   Relationship: Negative Feelings.)

Number 2 ONE WINS — BOTH LOSE
(Problem: Solution Found.   Relationship: Negative Feelings.)

Number 3 NO SOLUTION — BUT BOTH WIN
(Problem: Not Solved.   Relationship: Positive Feelings.)

Number 4 BOTH WIN
(Problem: Solution Found.   Relationship: Positive Feelings.)

Let's explore each of these four resolutions and evaluate the effectiveness of each. The let's examine what steps need to be taken to achieve result four — BOTH WIN.

four methods
by which couples resolve conflicts

Number 1 BOTH LOSE
(Problem: Not Solved   Relationship: Negative Feelings.)

When couples resolve their differences by this first method, both the

41

problem they are trying to solve and their feelings toward one another have a *negative* outcome. That is, they cannot find a solution to the problem they are faced with, and in addition they have argued or disagreed with one another in such a manner that they are hurt, angry and feeling resentful toward each other. In short, there are still bitter feelings between them. Obviously, not a desirable outcome.

Let's take a simple example to illustrate this first method. Bill and Barb want to see different movies, Bill an adventure story and Barb a romantic comedy. They argue and can't agree on which movie to see; in addition they argue in such a manner (attacking, putting-down, not listening) that they are hurting each other. They have not solved the problem — they still can't decide on which movie to see — and the manner in which they have communicated with one another has left both with unresolved and bitter feelings toward the other. This, then, is a negative outcome where BOTH PARTNERS LOSE. If most differences are settled via method one, couples probably don't stay together too long, or if they do, they're in for an unhappy relationship.

Number 2 ONE WINS — BOTH LOSE
(Problem: Solution Found.   Relationship: Negative Feelings.)

In this second method, unlike the first, partners make a decision on how to deal with the specific problem at hand. By hook or by crook, the parties find a method to deal with the problem, and come up with a solution. The methods employed to reach an agreement, however, have been detrimental to the relationship. As in the first method, there are still negative feelings between the couple because of the way in which they have communicated with each other. For example, they may have argued and yelled at one another, with neither listening to the other. In the first method, partners fail to find a solution to the problem, usually because both refuse to back down or give in to the other. In this second method, one partner usually gives in — a "peace at any price" solution. Such a surrender often occurs in a relationship where the partners have an unequal balance of power. Thus, the person with more power decides what the solution will be and the other acquiesces.

Let's go back to the example of Bill and Barb deciding which movie to see. If Bill has more power in the relationship than Barb has, it is quite likely he can coerce her into seeing the movie of his choice. She may reluctantly go along. This solution gives an appearance of harmony, but in the long run it will only generate a sense of resentment on Barb's part towards Bill. Barb will also have a feeling of hopelessness about controlling her own life. In turn, Bill will quite likely feel guilt and a lack of respect for Barb. The problem has been solved. The relationship is in jeopardy, however, if Bill and Barb commonly resolve their differences this way. With this method, then, we can say one partner may win the immediate skirmish, but ultimately BOTH LOSE, for in the long run this strategy destroys a relationship. The apparently quick solution to problems is offset by many negative feelings that undermine the quality of the mutual relationship between the partners.

Number 3 NO SOLUTION — BUT BOTH WIN
(Problem: Not Solved.   Relationship: Positive Feelings.)

In this method a decision can't be reached that pleases both partners. They don't find a solution at all or they find a solution that neither wants but will take because they can't find anything better. Unlike the previous two methods, however, in this resolution, there are *no* leftover negative feelings. The parties can't solve this problem to their mutual satisfaction, but they still feel good about each other in spite of their failure to do so.

What's happened here is that the way in which couples have communicated with one another has led to a positive outcome for their relationship. The underpinning of this method of conflict resolution is that both partners respect each other as people, respect each other's rights, and have an equitable balance of power between them. Neither has tried to manipulate or coerce the other into a solution either would later regret. They've worked hard to find a solution but haven't been able to come up with one both can agree on. They may accept a solution that neither is really happy with. The point is, though, they still have good, positive feelings towards each other. The relationship is still in good shape.

Let's go back to Bill and Barb. They can't agree on which movie to see and neither wants to see the other's first choice. They could pick a third movie, or see one movie tonight and the other choice another night, or not see a movie at all. The most important point here is that the respect they have for each other and their willingness to communicate openly and honestly have kept them close as two people. Since totally acceptable solutions to differences can't always be found, it's important not to let that failure control the relationship between people. Couples will always have arguments and differences. What is important is that they maintain a good feeling toward one another.

Number 4 BOTH WIN
(Problem: Solution Found   Relationship: Positive Feelings.)

In the fourth and last method, we have the ideal — a democratic agreement. A satisfactory solution is found to the problem and both partners have positive feelings toward one another. The methods a couple employ in solving the conflict result in their staying close. As with the third method, we are dealing here with a relationship of mutual respect marked by an equal balance of power, which leads to a spirit of fighting fairly. The result is an acceptable solution that both like, with no leftover hard feelings.

For Bill and Barb, the solution could be a third movie which both will like. Neither then would feel cheated. They have talked to each other in such a way that they have evidenced concern and respect for each other, so neither feels manipulated. When couples consistently resolve their differences using the BOTH WIN method, they both solve their problems and create positive feelings toward one another, thereby strengthening their relationship.

We stated earlier that to rejuvenate the feeling of love and maintain sexual compatibility, couples need to resolve their differences successfully. If conflicts are dealt with by methods one and two (BOTH LOSE or ONE WINS — ONE LOSES), the consequences will be bitter, hurt, and hostile feelings. Over time, these feelings turn couples off. Romantic feelings dissipate and sexual desire wanes. Clearly, the way to solve conflicts is by using methods three and four, since solving differences democratically and fighting fairly have broad implications for the overall quality of a relationship.

Part II/ learning to fight effectively

It's easy to see that methods of conflict resolution three and four are far better than methods one and two. The question is, what assurance is there that methods three and four will be employed? Wanting a democratic outcome where BOTH WIN is not the same as having it happen. Many people have entered an argument with the best of intentions to fight fairly and find a mutually acceptable solution, only to find within minutes that they're shouting and yelling at one another. Good intentions fly out the window, and the argument results in slamming of doors, pouting, and bitter feelings. What skills or steps are needed to iron out differences so that BOTH CAN WIN?

understanding anger

The first step in learning how to deal with conflict successfully is learning how to be assertive with your loved one. You need to be able to stand up to your partner and to display your real feelings. Since you have a conflict, more than likely these feelings are going to be negative. Though this step sounds simple, at a practical level it can become quite difficult. To understand the concept of being assertive, you need to start with understanding the dynamics of anger. Everybody gets angry when someone steps on his toes or does something unacceptable. Your partner may come home one hour late and spoil the surprise dinner you made, or flirt with your best friend at a cocktail party, or forget your birthday. These and a million other things can frustrate and annoy you and make you angry.

There are three phases in getting angry. The first is that you *experience* your anger. Initially, anger is experienced mostly at a physiological level. The heart beats faster, the pulse quickens, the stomach tightens; you're ready for a fight or flight response. The second phase in getting angry is at the psychological level. It is the *awareness* of anger. You can be aware or unaware of the anger you are experiencing. For example, suppose you share with several of your colleagues some important ideas in a new project that you have developed. Your colleagues are critical of your plans or proposal. You listen to their criticism and give, in return, logical counterarguments. At the time you are dealing with their criticism you are *not* aware of feeling angry; you rationalize that it's part of their job to evaluate and criticize your work. Several hours later though, when you're alone, you realize you're steaming mad. You're really burned up that your friends put down the project you had spent days developing. From this example we see that people are often not aware, at least initially, of the angry feelings they experience.

While is it important to be *aware* of your anger, a more crucial key is *acceptance* of anger as something normal and natural to human beings. One of the main reasons individuals don't become aware of angry feelings or have difficulty managing their anger is that, somewhere in their lives, they have learned that it's not proper to be angry. Most people want to see themselves (and have others see them) as sweet, kind, and loving, especially when dealing with a loved one. Getting angry is not considered consistent with being kind, sweet, and lovable. Therefore, many people contain their anger (unnaturally) or suffer from guilt feelings if they don't contain it. Everybody experiences anger, but many have not yet learned to be aware and accepting of that anger. An important step in resolving conflict is *acceptance* that angry feelings are normal.

The third phase in understanding anger centers on how people choose to *express* these negative feelings. As we remember from Chapter Two, people choose to express their anger in three basic ways: passively, assertively and aggressively. Of these, only being assertive is appropriate and useful in resolving conflict. To utilize anger most effectively in solving disagreements democratically, you need to be assertive. Assertiveness means you're honest and open with your negative feelings. You tell your partner how you really feel. You don't hide your anger, as you would do if you were passive, or attack or belittle your mate, as you would do if you were aggressive. Assertiveness is a direct, honest way to deal with your anger. You attempt to meet your needs but not at the expense of your partner. The needs of both should be met.

anger as a secondary emotion

In this chapter we have seen that becoming *aware* of your anger, *accep-*

ting anger as normal, and learning to *express* that anger in direct and honest terms are very important in resolving conflicts successfully. Something important to realize in understanding the dynamics of anger, however, is that anger can be a secondary emotion. Often, behind your anger lies a more *primary feeling*. People don't usually become aware of these primary, more vulnerable feelings until they are aware of and accepting of their anger.

Let's use some examples to illustrate this phenomenon. You are driving your car and another automobile swerves in front of you, almost hitting you. Instinctively you slam on the brakes, averting a head-on collision. You're safe and no one is injured. You are also steaming mad! You yell and scream at the other driver who almost killed you. After ventilating your anger you notice you are shaking and upset — you could have been killed! Behind your anger is *fear* and then *relief* that you are uninjured and alive. Behind your initial anger are other, more primary feelings: in this case, fear and then relief.

Take another example. You go to a cocktail party. After a few drinks, you see someone flirting with your mate. Your mate seems to be enjoying it and is flirting back! You're angry, and on the way home that night you give your partner a piece of your mind. You're mad, you know it, and you say so. After you have expressed your anger, however, you find the feelings you are experiencing are no longer anger but *jealousy*, the sense of being *threatened* by your mate's possible attraction to someone other than yourself. It is often true that you experience other, more vulnerable feelings behind your anger that also need to be shared.

The steps involved in dealing with anger then, are first, to become aware of and accept your angry feelings. Second, you must learn to express these feelings in an assertive manner and, third, to find if there are not more primary, vulnerable feelings behind your anger and, if so, to share these feelings as well. It's important to realize that if you don't first express your anger, then you probably won't become aware of the feelings behind it. Dealing in a direct manner with anger, then, is a first step for resolving conflict.

five steps to solving an argument

Step 1: Being Assertive

Now that we understand the phenomenon of anger better, it is easy to see the importance of being assertive in resolving conflict. The first step in resolving an argument is for both partners to be assertive. If you can't be assertive, you can't solve an argument so BOTH WIN. It's impossible. The first step is for each partner to share his or her angry feelings honestly and openly. Such sharing should be done in an assertive manner, with no withholding of feelings (being passive) and no attacking each other (being aggressive). Passive and aggressive methods of confrontation only lead to more problems. Direct, honest assertion about what is bothering you is a first and critical step. An example will help to illustrate the importance of this first step. Sharon sees that Mike does not help out with the household chores. Since both she and Mike work full time, though, she feels the housework should be a shared responsibility.

> *Sharon:* "Mike, I am frustrated and angry with your behavior. I feel like I have the responsibility for all the housecleaning and I don't think it's fair. I think we should share it."
>
> *Mike·* "Well, I'm working two jobs now and I feel you should do more of the work at home than I do. I'm making up for it with the two jobs I've got."

We see in this simple example that both people are being assertive and are sharing their feelings. Being assertive by itself doesn't solve their problem, but it gets the problem-solving process off on the right foot. The reason is that both are getting off their chests what they feel and think. You can't solve a problem unless you are willing to talk openly about what is going on inside you. If you do so in an assertive manner (by sharing anger and the more primary feelings behind the anger), each of you knows where the other stands. Also, no one is likely to get overly-defensive since neither person has been attacked and put down.

Step 2: Listening

It's important for both partners to be assertive and get their feelings off their chests; that way each knows where the other stands. Even when you are assertive, though, your mate will probably react with some defensiveness. No one likes to be criticized or confronted, no matter how tactfully or honestly it is done. A major difficulty when you get into an argument or discussion with your loved one is that the confrontation can quickly escalate and get out of control. Both of you can start out being assertive, but if you get defensive because your mate is criticizing you, you tend to grow more and more assertive until one or both of you has become aggressive. Sometimes, if both people get aggressive, a shouting match results. Or if just one partner becomes aggressive, the other withdraws and either gives in unwillingly or pouts and sulks. Either way, this escalation leads to a breakdown in communication and prevents couples from solving their differences democratically.

To stop this escalation before it starts, partners need to learn to *listen effectively.* If you listen carefully to someone and make it clear that you understand what he or she is saying, your behavior generally has a calming effect. When someone really listens to you, you feel that you have been heard and understood, and you become less argumentative, less defensive, and more willing to stop arguing and to listen in return. Effective listening is a two-step process: first, you take the time and effort to concentrate on what someone is saying to you; second, you then restate back to the other person the essence of what you hear him or her trying to communicate. Let's go back to the example of Mike and Sharon and the issue of household chores.

> *Sharon:* (assertive confrontation)
> "Mike, I am frustrated and angry with your behavior. I feel like I have the responsibility for all the housecleaning and I don't think it's fair. I think we should share this."
>
> *Mike* (listening)
> "You feel that you're getting cheated and I am not holding up my half of the bargain."
>
> *Sharon:* "Yes, that's true."
>
> *Mike:* (assertive confrontation)
> "Well, I am working two jobs now and I feel you should do more of the work at home. I am making up for it with the two jobs I've got."
>
> *Sharon:* (listening)
> "You feel that you're doing half the work by having not one but two jobs. Is that it?
>
> *Mike:* "Yes."

In this exchange we see that *listening* and *assertion* go hand-in-hand. Careful listening allows you to make sure that you really hear what your loved one is saying. When you first, pay attention so that you really hear what your loved one is saying and, second, restate what you heard him or her telling you, it proves to the other person that you have heard him or her accurately. Before you get defensive or disagree with your spouse or loved one, be reasonably sure that you have heard the message correctly. Check it out by listening. *Most arguments escalate and get out of control because partners haven't really heard what the other has said, and/or have misinterpreted it.*

Steps 1 and 2, being assertive and listening, can be repeated over and over as couples hash out their feelings. A rule of thumb to follow during the initial stages of conflict is: Don't restate your own argument before you have first listened to your partner and reflected back what your partner has said to you to his or her satisfaction. After that, you may agree, disagree, express your own point of view, etc. As long as you remember to follow this simple rule, you will keep the lines of communication open between you and your loved one. As you go back and forth, being assertive as well as listening to each other, you both have a chance to let the other know what is bothering you as well as proving you understand how he or she feels. Repeated as many times as needed, these two skills help keep heads cool, and also lead to the third step to solving an argument.

Step 3: Definition of the Problem

Once couples have stated how they feel and aired both sides of the story, agreement on a definition of the problem should be possible. It might help to understand better the idea of *definition* of the *problem* by noting two ways in which problems can be identified. The problem may be identified in specific *behavioral terms* (i.e., who does the housework), or it may be identified as a *personality trait* or *characteristic* (i.e., you are a sloppy housekeeper). *As a general rule, it is better to define the problem in specific behavior terms rather than in terms of personality of one or the other person.* When you define the problem in terms of the other's personality (i.e., "you're not thoughtful," "you're such an inconsiderate person," "you don't care about anyone but yourself," etc.), you can only make him or her defensive and angry at you. Nonproductive arguments usually result which do not generally resolve conflicts in a helpful or healthy way. Returning to the example of Sharon and Mike, they may define their problem as household chores (*not* a personality trait) and specifically how many each of them should be responsible for. Once the problem has been defined to *both* people's satisfaction, a couple can move on to the fourth step.

Step 4: Finding Possible Solutions

To enter into this stage of conflict resolution, you need to feel relaxed and at ease with yourself and your partner. The primary goal at this stage is to come up with as many solutions to the problem as possible. Back to the example of Mike and Sharon. They generated to following list of possible solutions to the problem of household chores:

1. Mike does all the chores (Sharon's idea).
2. Sharon does all the chores (Mike's idea).
3. No one does the chores.
4. Divide the chores 50/50.
5. Sharon does more of the chores until Mike's second job terminates in about six weeks. After that, they will go 50/50 on the chores.
6. Hire a maid to do the housework.

In this fourth step, you'll want to start out by simply generating ideas without evaluating them. Evaluation of each idea as it is proposed cuts off the creative flow of suggestions. The reason is obvious: as soon as one of your ideas has been criticized, you will stop coming up with any more. So, come up with as many ideas as possible. The time for evaluation comes after you're all done "brainstorming" ideas.

49

Step 5: Deciding on a Solution

This fifth and final step comes after you have developed as long and complete a list of ideas as possible. Now you need to go back over the list to find one or two workable ideas and see if you can agree on one. This step requires the art of compromise and the willingness to find a workable solution. Both partners need to realize that they will not get everything that they want. In the case of Mike and Sharon and the household chores, they decided on a combination of two ideas they had generated. They agreed that Sharon would take the responsibility for more of the housework for six weeks until Mike's second job terminated. Then they would go 50/50 on the household duties. They would also hire a maid for those six weeks to help Sharon, however, so that she wouldn't be overwhelmed with an excessive amount of housework. Mike would pay the maid's salary. Mike and Sharon found a solution both could live with. The result: BOTH WIN.

When the inevitable conflicts that come up are resolved in this manner, couples feel good about themselves and have little or no resentment toward each other. In fact, they become closer as a couple. To summarize the five steps to achieving a positive outcome — BOTH WIN:

1. Be assertive (state feelings honestly, don't attack partner).
2. Listen (make sure you hear how mate feels).
3. Define the problem (in behavioral terms).
4. Generate a list of alternatives (brainstorm ideas but don't evaluate them).
5. Pick a solution (find a solution both can live with).

dealing with a crisis

This section on conflict resolution is to aid you in dealing with the ongoing, day-to-day conflicts all couples face and must address. At one time or another, however, most couples experience a crisis in their relationship. One person or another may threaten to end the relationship or may in fact do so. A number of factors can spark a crisis for a couple.

John and Cheryl had been dating for several years and planned on marrying. Five months prior to coming for counseling, John had been laid off his construction job. Over the next few months, he spent his time doing odd jobs around the house, drinking more, and growing increasingly more depressed. One night after John had been drinking heavily, he and Cheryl got in an argument. Under most circumstances when they argued, they'd yell, shout at each other and go to their separate apartments to cool off for several hours. This time, however, John, inebriated, frustrated and angry, physically beat Cheryl up. Cheryl required emergency medical treatment as a result of several cuts and lacerations. In their three-year relationship John had never hit Cheryl, let alone physically abused her.

This unfortunate incident precipitated a crisis in their relationship. Cheryl felt hurt, angry and fearful of John. "He showed me he could be a monster." John felt guilt and remorse for his behavior and couldn't understand why he had done something so unlike himself.

Working through a crisis, a couple needs first to understand what caused the crisis. In this case, John's being laid off work and feeling unproductive in his life were contributing factors to his physically abusing his girlfriend. John needed to come to some understanding of why he had behaved the way he had so he could control it in the future. He also needed to begin to forgive himself in order to alleviate some of his overwhelming guilt. Cheryl needed to understand John's recent depression due to his job difficulties. Over time, she also had to allow herself to trust John again and eventually to forgive him.

Both partners needed to work harder at their relationship to ensure that another such incident would not happen again. Sometimes in crisis, couples need to seek professional help to insure the likelihood that the crisis will ultimately be resolved positively. Dealing with a crisis requires patience, understanding and a determination to work hard on the relationship.

summary

Conflict, fights, and arguments are inevitable parts of a love relationship. Rarely can a couple say, "We never fight." Most do now and will in the future. The critical issue is not that they fight, but *how* they fight. If they learn to fight fairly and honestly, most differences can be resolved in a democratic BOTH WIN manner. Our constructive model for resolving conflicts requires a commitment by both parties to accept anger and share feelings in an assertive manner, and to follow through with the five steps of Problem Solving. As with other areas we have discussed, resolving conflicts successfully brings couples together and makes for strong, healthier relationships.

5

developing emotional intimacy

introduction

Up to this point, we have explored the feeling of love, interpersonal communication skills, sexual compatibility, and methods of conflict. In these next two chapters we want to deal with the issue of friendship. Couples need to be friends as well as lovers. The feeling of love wanes a bit over time so that sexual attraction is not usually as strong and intense as it was early in the relationship. The day-to-day realities of a relationship (job, children, housework, bills) take some of the "spark" out of a relationship. If couples can learn to become close friends, however, they can strengthen their relationship and give greater satisfaction to one another.

two elements of friendship

I believe friendship can best be understood if broken down into two broad areas. One aspect of being a friend has to do with intimacy. Intimacy means sharing yourself as a person, feeling free to be who you really are without pretense or disguise. This aspect of friendship allows you to share yourself more completely with another person. Friends share the more vulnerable side of themselves, those aspects of personality and behavior they aren't sure they fully accept or like themselves. Friends also share their more positive aspects, their successes, accomplishments, and joys. It is the freedom to share at a deep and intimate level that makes people friends.

A second aspect of being friends is having fun together, being able to play with one another. It's being able to relax and enjoy yourselves and to spend positive and enjoyable time with one another. When you were a child, you had fun with friends doing such things as riding bikes, going swimming, play-ing tag, sewing, playing war. As adults you talk, sail, go to movies, play tennis, make love. These two areas, the capacity for intimacy and the ability to have fun together, make up the substance of friendship. In this chapter we're going to explore the area of emotional intimacy and in the following chapter we'll examine fun and play. Our goal is to understand how couples can grow closer to each other on an emotionally intimate level and enhance the good times they have together. The result will be the building of a mutually rewarding friendship.

what is emotional intimacy?

As we stated earlier, emotional intimacy refers to the ability to be open and honest and to be fully yourself with your partner. It is being able to share all facets of yourself. One side of intimacy, then, is being able to be yourself. The other side of emotional intimacy is being able to accept your partner as a human being as uncritically as possible. If you can achieve these two things, you will feel a close, loving bond with your mate.

how do we become intimate?

Both sharing yourself and learning about your loved one as a person will lead to intimacy. How do you accomplish this goal? What specific steps can be taken to get closer to those you love? Learning to be intimate first requires making a *commitment* to be intimate, setting this as a personal goal for your-self. What such a commitment means on a practical level is that you must be willing to take the risk of being yourself. To do so you need to know and accept yourself as a person. For many people, sharing themselves can be a fearful undertaking because at times they must deal with their mate's not liking some aspect of themselves. Therefore you may have to risk being honest in the face of disapproval and at times rejection. Such self-disclosure can indeed be frightening.

You also need to make a commitment to know and to meet the needs of your loved one. To do so will take time, patience, effort, and some sacrifices on your part.

How do we go about sharing ourselves and meeting the needs of our loved one? In addition to the commitment to intimacy, you will need specific skills to achieve your goal of forming a close, loving bond with your partner. In Chapter Two we looked at two interpersonal skills (Giving and Assertion) that are important skills for forming a successful love relationship. We saw in the last chapter on conflict that the Assertion skill plays a critical role in the ability to solve problems democratically. Now we shall see that these and other interpersonal skills will help you to form a more intimate relationship with the one you love. As you recall, Assertion skills allow you to look after your own interests and to prevent others from taking advantage of you. The capacity to Give, on the other hand, allows you to help meet the needs of others. These skills are not only critical in forming a successful relationship, but once the relationship is formed, they will allow it to develop on a deeper level. In addition to Giving and Assertion, two other skills will now help you to form a more intimate relationship with your loved one. These two skills are the ability to be *Self-Disclosing* and the ability to be a good *Listener*. Let's start by looking at Self-Disclosure.

self-disclosure

The "self" is the subjective part of every individual — his or her intimate thoughts, feelings, fantasies, values, daydreams, and needs. In short, the self is the inner person who is not automatically available to a loved one, or to any-one else for that matter. In fact, others can know what goes on inside you from either the inferences they make about you or from your sharing your "self" with them. This process of sharing yourself with another person is called self-disclosure.

Self-disclosure is very important as a means of establishing intimacy in a relationship. It's really the best way your partner can form a reasonably accurate picture of who you are as a person, and it's hard to form a love rela-tionship without knowing someone well. Therefore, disclosure is one of the best means of getting close to your mate. Self-disclosure is also a way of get-ting to know yourself better. As you share yourself with someone you love and trust, you begin to reach a better understanding of yourself. Research also shows that the ability of people to be self-disclosing is related to a healthy per-sonality and a positive self-concept.

Self-disclosure varies in nature from that involving little or no personal risk to that which is very personal and intimate. You can talk about such things as a hobby, the weather, who's going to win the Super Bowl with little or no personal risk. Or you can discuss more intimate topics, such as a personal problem, a painful failure, fears, hopes, and aspirations, that are more reveal-ing of the real you inside.

As you share at a greater depth, the risks seem greater. It will hurt more if you are rejected or ignored by someone you love. The rewards are also greater, however, for such sharing creates a close, loving bond between men and women. When you withhold yourself and don't share at an intimate level, you end up playing roles with your partner, hiding behind a facade which often leads to dishonesty and deceit. Self-disclosure, then, is a necessary interpersonal skill that every person needs to develop to become more intimate with a loved one.

An exercise you may wish to try with your partner is to take an hour a day for several weeks to practice self-disclosure. The goal of this hour is to pick different topics of individual and mutual interest and then take turns sharing your feelings on them. The topics can be of your own choosing; other couples have chosen such subjects as politics, sexual preferences, career goals, attitudes toward parents. Simply pick topics that are relevant to you both. The goal is not to judge yourself or your mate, but rather to listen and to share your feelings and ideas.

It may be easier to see the importance of honest and intimate self-disclosure if we look at a case history. Ron and Laura had been married for a year and a half when they came for counseling. Laura described the problem as a lack of closeness between her and Ron. During their courtship of eight months, everything had been wonderful. She and Ron talked all the time and shared all aspects of their lives, she reported. They enjoyed each other's company and did many enjoyable things together — fishing, bowling, going out to dinner. The main reason she fell in love with Ron and wanted to marry him, she said, was because of the time they spent talking and sharing themselves with each other. Within six months after they had married, however, Laura claimed that they rarely had long talks anymore. Most evenings Ron watched television while Laura read or sewed. When she tried to engage Ron in conversation, he usually withdrew, saying he was tired after work and just wanted to relax and be alone. This became the pattern in their marriage: Ron withdrew in the evenings to the television and Laura was left by herself. At first, Laura argued and picked fights with Ron, hoping to change his behavior, but Ron perceived her behavior as nagging and only withdrew more. Finally, Laura gave up and she herself withdrew into a stormy silence.

Ron stated that he too had been quite happy with their courtship, and that during that time he had been very close to Laura. He added that though he loved Laura he also like to spend considerable amounts of time alone. He was happy and content to be by himself, and watching television was a favorite way of being alone for him. Ron was very put off by Laura's angry outbursts at him over his television watching. He disliked fighting and arguing so much that he just withdrew, seeing withdrawal as his only defense. The results were angry and hurt feelings on both sides and a loss of closeness they had felt earlier in their relationship.

As it turned out, Ron was fearful of fighting, and the initial stages of therapy were directed to helping him deal more directly with his anger. As a result, both Ron and Laura learned to deal more openly and honestly with their conflicts. Ron was still quite undisclosing as a person, however. His history revealed a family environment both permissive and neglectful, in which the children were allowed a considerable amount of freedom to do as they pleased. His family was not particularly close or self-disclosing, and Ron had little experience in this area. During Ron's and Laura's courtship, strong feelings of Romantic Love moved Ron to be more self-disclosing than he had ever been in his life. Now that Romantic Love had worn off, though, and they were truly "married," Ron had gone back to his old style of keeping to himself. Self-disclosure made him uncomfortable.

At first, it was hard for Ron to open up and share himself, both in therapy and with his wife. A contract the couple worked out in therapy helped them immensely. Several nights a week Ron was allowed to watch television and be alone the entire evening. He didn't have to feel guilty or feel that he was displeasing Laura in some way by doing so. These evenings were his time to be alone and to enjoy himself. The other part of the contract called for Laura and Ron to spend an evening together (without television), talking, fixing dinner together, having some wine. They were to relax and enjoy themselves and get to know each other a bit better.

At first, Ron reported he felt awkward and ill at ease during the evening with Laura, not knowing what to talk about besides work and household matters. On the other hand, Laura was able to share herself fairly easily. She had come from a close, loving home, in which people talked a great deal about their lives. The result was that Laura was already comfortable with self-disclosure and able to be a good role model for Ron. Over time Ron began to loosen up and share more of himself at a personal level. To his surprise, he found that Laura was not only interested in him but most accepting of him as well. As he showed more of himself Ron found that he was more in touch with himself and understood himself better and over a period of four to six months, Ron and Laura's relationship changed and grew. Ron will probably never be as open and self-disclosing as Laura — and he still likes to have a considerable amount of time to himself — but their relationship is quite different now and they both are happier with each other.

In this example, we see that Self-Disclosure at a deep level meets a need all individuals have: the human need for closeness and intimacy. From sharing yourself more openly, you usually learn and understand more about yourself, and become closer to those you love and care about. Many individuals, such as Ron, are nervous about sharing, fearing they will not be accepted or will perhaps even be rejected. Sometimes these fears have some basis in reality. As a child you may have been ignored or rejected by a parent; as an adult you may have been "burned" in a relationship by someone you loved. These negative experiences, therefore, can make you cautious about opening up and sharing the more vulnerable aspects of yourself. The more you can be self-disclosing with your mate, however, the more self-disclosing your partner will be with you. And the closer you will become.

learning to listen

Listening, seeing things from the other person's point of view, and being accepting of your partner are great ways to encourage Self-Disclosure. In Chapter Two and in the previous chapter, we noted that Listening was one of the skills that help form a successful love relationship. Knowing how to Listen allows you to know the other person. When you really Listen to someone in the initial stages of a relationship, you find out about the other person's likes, dislikes, and values. Once a relationship is formed, being an effective Listener serves several different functions, strengthening the relationship and making it more intimate. When you really Listen to your partner you communicate your genuine interest and concern. You show that you care about your loved one by putting aside your interests and taking the time to be with him or her.

Listening can also be a powerful therapeutic tool when your partner wants to talk about a personal problem and needs someone to listen. Being a concerned Listener leads to healing some of the inevitable pains and hurts encountered in life. Your Listening will also make it easier for your mate to be self-disclosing.

Let's use another case example to illuminate how important being able to Listen is to a relationship. Dick and Jenny have been married for twenty years and have three teenage children. Dick is a successful businessman and Jenny has been a homemaker for most of their marriage. In the last few years, as the children have gotten older, Jenny has taken a part-time job doing volunteer work at a local hospital. At Jenny's insistence, Dick and she came for therapy. They saw therapy as a last resort, since Jenny had already filed for a divorce. Dick had resisted counseling in the past, feeling it would be a waste of time. Now, however, frightened by Jenny's threat of divorce, he came willingly for treatment. He stated he very much wanted to remain married to Jenny.

Dick came from a home where achievement was strongly stressed. He was hard-working, like his father, and earned an almost straight-A average in both high school and college. He had become quite successful in business because of his dedication to his career. He worked long hours at the office and always brought work home as well. Dick believed in firm discipline with the children; by most standards he would be considered autocratic. Though he said he loved Jenny, he spent little time with her and seemed to have little awareness of her emotional needs.

Jenny grew up in a more emotionally supportive environment than Dick's. She was close to her parents and siblings. Jenny had always been supportive of Dick's career, even willing to have their marriage take a back seat to his career and his other interests. In recent years, though, with the children growing older and with Jenny going back to work, she had begun to feel that Dick was not filling many of her emotional needs. Jenny's major complaint about him was that Dick was "so unemotional;" a conversation with Dick was like a business meeting — matter-of-fact, to the point, and short. Dick never seemed to have time to relax and just talk. In terms of the interpersonal skills we have explored, Dick had no problem being Assertive; in fact, he was oftentimes aggressive. He was Self-Disclosing but in an unemotional manner. He was Giving but usually with presents that people had not asked for and often neither wanted nor needed. Dick's greatest problem was his inability to Listen and really hear others. Dick liked to make decisions for himself and others; if there was no immediate objection raised, he charged forward, doing what he wanted. Since Jenny was somewhat passive, Dick pretty much ran the show.

Some time in therapy was devoted to teaching Jenny some basic Assertive skills, so that she could feel on a more equal footing with her husband. She needed to learn to make her desires known to Dick so that she could get her needs met on a consistent basis. For Dick, a major focus in therapy was helping him learn how to Listen to others. Teaching Dick specific Listening skills, namely facilitative listening (reflecting the feelings and the essence of another's message), was relatively easy; Dick was bright and learned quickly. Getting Dick to practice and use the facilitative listening skill on a consistent basis was the hard part. He simply wanted to give others his advice and then to get on with things. Over time, though, Dick learned to slow down and be more patient. He also learned to Listen to his wife and children. Results were gradual but significant; Dick really began to hear what other people were saying to him.

An incident occurred several months after Dick had begun using Listening skills to illustrate how important this skill is to developing intimacy. Jenny had tired of her volunteer job but had not yet decided what to do next. She was in quite a bit of inner turmoil, trying to decide whether she should work at all and, if so, in what kind of job. In the past, when Jenny had had problems, Dick had either ignored her or, in his impatient, gruff manner, had given her some hasty, poorly thought-out advice. This time, however, he sat down and really listened. He heard Jenny's fears about seeking employment for the first time in twenty years, her doubts about her adequacy in the area of achievement, and her confusion as to what type of job or schooling she should seek. For the first time in a long while, Jenny felt listened to by her husband. Dick also felt he really heard and was supportive of Jenny. This incident and other interactions like it over time brought Dick and Jenny closer together. Dick grew a little less autocratic with the children and more responsive to his wife's emotional needs. As time passed, Dick reported that he felt he knew his family better and, further, that he was beginning to know them as people. He also reported experiencing closer, more loving feelings towards his wife and children. Jenny felt closer to Dick, too, and felt that he was more aware of her needs and responsive to them. Dick made no major personality change but his learning to Listen and Jenny's acquisition of some Assertive skills helped both to relate more effectively to each other.

giving — self-disclosure and listening

Both effective Listening and genuine Self-Disclosure bring couples closer. These skills increase couples' communication and understanding. Learning to Give, like Self-Disclosure and effective Listening, also fosters closer, more loving relationships. In Chapter Two we introduced the concept of Giving and discussed its role in a love relationship. We saw that Giving and the ability to be Assertive are interpersonal skills necessary for the development of a successful love relationship. Use of these two skills lets couples meet each other's needs and their own needs as well. Giving and Assertiveness facilitate formation of a healthy and equal relationship and each reinforces the effectiveness of the other.

Couples find it easier to Give effectively when each knows what the other wants or needs. If you want something of your partner — a night away from the children, time to talk, a special favor — you need to be Self-Disclosing about your needs. Far too often individuals expect the spouse to be a mindreader. If you only hint around or, worse yet, just *expect* something without giving any hints at all, you rarely receive the gifts and favors you want. We need to be Assertive and Self-Disclosing of needs or others will have difficulty meeting them.

If you are to Give effectively, your mate has to be Self-Disclosing and you have to Listen and Respond. Again, let's illustrate with a case example.

Todd and Tina have been married for six years and have two small children. Todd is a high school teacher and Tina is a guidance counselor. They have two basic problems: first, they have difficulty fighting fairly. Both are reluctant to fight. Instead, they deal with their anger in passive, nonassertive ways and in indirectly aggressive ways, by withholding love and favors from one another. This behavior gave rise to their second problem: neither Gives openly and freely to the other. Unable to manage conflict effectively and not giving to one another, both are frustrated and lonely in their marriage. Each needed training in how to deal with conflict in a more assertive manner; early therapy sessions were devoted to assertion training.

As Todd and Tina began to be more honest and Assertive with one another, they began to feel closer and more trusting in their relationship. In the last several years, however, because they had not dealt directly with their anger, they had found indirect ways to punish one another. These methods usually involved withholding love and not Giving what the other wanted. In this situation, Tina had gained weight and now evinced little interest in sex. Both the weight gain and her lack of interest in sex angered Todd. Todd, too, had begun to withhold affection. He had stopped Giving to Tina by not doing those small but special things she liked, such as remembering her birthday or their anniversary.

Learning to Give means meeting the other person's needs. What Giving this couple had been doing had been Giving Out of Obligation, which only brought them more frustration and resentment. They now needed to learn to Give Tit for Tat (see Chapter Two). Each needed to make an active attempt to meet the other's needs, while also expecting his or her own needs to be met. Over a three to four month period, Tina lost weight and regained her interest in sex. As a result, Todd felt that Tina was doing something he wanted, and he felt cared about. Todd also learned to Give to Tina, taking time to meet her emotional needs, listening to her, and remembering her birthday and their anniversary by making them special events. The result was that Tina felt appreciated and valued. This Tit for Tat Giving led, over time, to more mutual trust and commitment to each other. As a result, they were able to begin Giving From the Heart.

The results of Todd and Tina's Giving were twofold: first, they learned that Giving begets Giving. The more freely they gave to each other, the more comfortable each felt Giving to each other. Second, they found when they gave to each other something they valued as important, both felt appreciated and cared about. Each began to feel special and significant in the other's life.

summary

Giving, taking the time to Listen, and genuine Self-Disclosure are three things that help to form a more intimate bond between a couple. When couples do these things in a sincere, honest way, they become closer and more deeply involved. The use of these skills creates an environment in which couples can know each other on a deeper, more meaningful, and more intimate level.

6

developing positive time together

introduction

In the previous chapter we saw that one aspect of building friendship with another was developing the capacity for emotional intimacy. The achievement of intimacy usually requires a major effort and involves taking risks and being more vulnerable on a personal level. Now we want to examine another aspect of friendship — having fun with and enjoying your partner.

the concept of conflict-free time

One aspect of being a friend has to do with spending positive, enjoyable time with the one you love. To have a happy relationship you have to enjoy being with your mate and doing fun things together. A prerequisite to spending time enjoyably, either alone or with someone, is the absence of problems in your life at that particular time. Thus, neither of you is experiencing any present difficulty in your personal life (i.e., you are not bored, sad, depressed, worried), and each of you finds the other's behavior acceptable (i. e., neither is doing anything to interfere with meeting the other's needs). At such a juncture, a relationship is *conflict-free*. Conflict-free time occurs when neither of you has a problem and both feel good about each other. Conflict-free time is the key to having good times together.

types of conflict-free time

The time couples can spend enjoyably, experiencing no problems and meeting their needs for fun/play and leisure, falls into three categories: Individual Time, Qualitative Time, and Diffused Time.

Individual Time. Individual Time refers to those times when you are by yourself, separate from others. It is time ALONE, away from other people, devoted to activities that are enjoyable, relaxing, and rewarding. This time is structured differently by each person. Some activities might include reading a book, going for a walk, engaging in a craft, having a coffee break, daydreaming, drawing, or jogging. Individual-time activities can run the gamut from activities that are just plain fun to something involving personal growth and self-fulfillment. The significant aspect of Individual Time is that you meet your need for time alone, away from your mate and other people. The main characteristics of Individual Time are:

1. Individuals are fulfilled by doing something enjoyable away from others.
2. During this time, there is little or no contact between partners.
3. This lack of contact is acceptable to both partners.

The major benefit of Individual Time is that it is an opportunity to avoid interaction with other people. Since much of life is spent in complex human interactions, momentarily retiring from this constant interaction can be enjoyable and regenerative in nature. Engaging in adequate amounts of Individual Time also meets a basic need to understand yourself, to process the day's activities, to enjoy yourself, and to relax.

It appears that getting adequate amounts of Individual Time is necessary for mental well-being. When you don't have enough Individual Time, you may begin to feel tense, unable to relax, or overwhelmed by occurrences in your environment. Also, insufficient time alone may result in increased impatience, irritation, or anger at others. Finally, lack of Individual Time for solitude and reflection may minimize the opportunity for you to get to know yourself better.

Unfortunately, few people deliberately provide many opportunities for themselves to engage in Individual Time. It might help to understand Individual Time better if you jot down five to ten things you like to do alone, all by yourself. Then ask yourself, are you getting enough Individual Time for these activities? Also, are there other possible ways of spending some Individual Time that you have not tried or have not done lately because you have been too busy? It's important to remember that Individual Time is something everyone needs on a regular basis.

I first got interested in Individual Time a number of years ago when I was conducting training programs for parents. I found many young mothers, at home all day with two or three children with husbands to deal with in the evening, were complaining of never having any time to be by themselves. For them, being a parent was a twenty-four-hour-a-day job. Even providing them with effective parenting skills to deal with their children was not enough. After I explained the concept of Individual Time and asked these young women to keep a record of how much time they had alone during the week, I found they had little or no Individual Time! Once these mothers started taking time out for themselves, doing things alone away from the children and their spouses, they reported feeling more relaxed and at ease with themselves. They also reported that the everyday hassles of parenthood were easier to deal with.

The things the young mothers did were often quite simple, such as taking a long hot bath, going for a bike ride, reading a book, taking a nap. But these activities gave them a chance to be by themselves and to "recharge their batteries." Individual Time, then, is a necessity for everyone. Often people get so busy with work or so involved in meeting the needs of others that they forget about taking some time for themselves, seeing it as being selfish and self-indulgent. You need to recognize that it is a normal, natural thing to be alone. You may also need the cooperation of your loved one, especially if you have children. Couples need to have time to be by themselves. It can often help you to appreciate your mate more, when you are apart for a while.

If you don't get adequate amounts of Individual Time, you often grow cross and irritable at those you love. Your level of tolerance goes down dramatically. When you have time alone to engage in enjoyable and rewarding activities, you are not only easier to live with but happier and more content with yourself. The amount of Individual Time needed may vary for each individual. The important thing, though, is to take that time alone on a regular basis, doing things you like.

Qualitative Time. The second type of conflict-free time is called Qualitative Time. Whereas Individual Time provides for your need for solitude, personal growth, and enjoyment ALONE, Qualitative Time meets your need for TOGETHERNESS. It is a time wherein you interact with your loved one in a positive, enjoyable way; in short, it is a time for fun together. The focus is on the QUALITY of the interaction rather than on the amount of time spent together.

Qualitative Time is when both partners are accepting of one another and are truly enjoying each other's company. To make the best use of this time, it is necessary to put aside extraneous thoughts and to become meaningfully involved in the present moment with your partner. The activities in which you can engage with your loved one are many: talking, making love, bike riding, playing a game, walking together, having dinner together. If both of you regard the time as enjoyable and meaningful, it's Qualitative Time. The main characteristics of Qualitative Time are:

1. Qualitative Time is an interaction between just TWO people.
2. Both partners interact with one another, engaging in an activity that BOTH enjoy.
3. Both partners fulfill their needs together to their mutual satisfaction.
4. Both partners have caring, loving feelings for each other and a sense of satisfaction and enjoyment with themselves.
5. The partners are totally involved with each other, to the exclusion of all else. They ignore extraneous thoughts and distractions, focusing on the here and now. Each gets the other's undivided attention.

One of the major benefits of Qualitative Time is that it both meets the need for close human contact and provides an avenue for affirmation of selfhood. Qualitative Time also provides an opportunity to get to know each other and to help each other grow. Qualitative Time strengthens the relationship and is one of the best ways of building a healthy relationship and bringing couples closer together. Finally, because Qualitative Time encourages a strong, positive relationship between people, it makes it easier for them to deal with the inevitable conflicts that occasionally arise.

A useful exercise here is to list four or five things you have done with your loved one in the last several weeks that you would define as Qualitative Time. Remember that Qualitative Time is not defined by the amount of time spent together but by the quality of your interaction with your mate. Sometimes just a five to ten minute intimate talk between loved ones is Qualitative Time. After you have made your list, try to determine what it was about an experience that made it Qualitative for both of you.

Another useful exercise is to list those things you would like to do with your mate, things you consider of a Qualitative nature, but which you haven't done at all or haven't done for a long time. Then give these new activities a try and see how they turn out. Many times this exercise is a way to broaden your repertoire of things to do.

The more positive Qualitative Time you spend with your partner, the more you develop common interests. Common interests give you things you and your mate can do together. Couples usually enter into relationships with a successful history of individual interests. A man may already like to play golf and tennis and to go to football games. When their relationship begins, a woman may already enjoy sewing, bowling, and attending the opera. Each has individual interests that provide pleasure and enjoyment. When individuals get involved, they need to develop interests they can share. Such interests maximize opportunities for Qualitative Time. Sometimes you can take up one or more of your loved one's interests. For instance, a wife might learn to play tennis so that she can enjoy a sport her husband has already played and enjoyed for some years. Or he could take up bowling and join the league she has played in for a long time. Couples often find it is easier to start fresh, taking up something neither has done before, so that they can learn together. A new interest eliminates the situation of one being the "expert," having to show the other "how to do it," which often creates its own problems of frustration and impatience.

My interest in Qualitative Time, like my interest in Individual Time, grew out of my work with young parents. I found that when parents spent Qualitative Time with their children, doing such things as reading together, playing games, wrestling and talking, their relationship improved significantly. For Qualitative Time to be effective, a parent had to spend time alone with just *one* child, so that the child would get the parent's undivided attention. In addition, their activity has to be mutually satisfying. For instance, the time a bored father with a business problem on his mind spent pushing his daughter on her swing set would not qualify as Qualitative Time. Rather, the parent had to be actively involved in the task and having fun too. When these requirements for Qualitative Time were met, I found that several positive things occurred. First, children who got adequate amounts of Qualitative Time were more willing to spend time on their own, away from their parents. This time gave the parents, especially mothers, needed breaks for some Individual Time. Also, children didn't seem to create as many problems for their parents as they had previously, and the problems that did arise seemed easier to resolve because Qualitative Time had helped build a positive relationship between parents and child. Finally, the overall quality of the parent-child relationship improved.

I also trained schoolteachers in the use of Qualitative Time and found similar results. As I began to work with couples, I found that many of them spent very little Qualitative Time together. Problems in their relationship or just the day-to-day hassles of life consumed most of the time left after work and taking care of the children. As with teachers and parents, couples trained in Qualitative Time were brought closer together and their relationships improved.

It may help to see just how important this type of time is if we examine what happens when people don't get enough Qualitative Time. All human beings need attention and recognition from others. There are three basic types of attention or recognition we receive or give: *positive attention, negative attention,* or *no attention.* Positive attention correlates roughly to Qualitative Time — you give others your positive interest and involvement. Negative attention refers to your negative reaction to people who do things which irritate you. For example, when you discipline a child, the child has done something to get your negative attention. Your discipline is negative and adverse, but it is still a form of attention. Finally, there is no attention — simply being ignored.

All people prefer positive attention as a first choice; very few people like to be ignored by those they love. In my work with parents, teachers, and couples, I found that if people didn't get enough Qualitative Time (positive attention), they quickly begin to try to get some negative attention in one of two ways. First, a child, student or mate might develop personal problems to get attention, such as complaints that "I am sick, I don't feel up to going to work (or school)" or "I am depressed today, have nothing to do. Please come talk to me." Second, a child, student or loved one might do things to irritate a parent, spouse or teacher, knowing that this behavior would lead to an angry outburst. Even though this attention was quite negative, it was seen as better than being ignored. Thus, everyone needs Qualitative Time or they will develop problems for themselves or for others in the attempt to get some kind of time and attention. Many couples fight with each other just to get some attention, even if it is negative, from their mates. Oftentimes, when couples work to increase their positive Qualitative Time, their arguments and fights decrease dramatically.

I have treated many couples who felt their relationship problems were severe and that there was little they could do to improve their situation. Often with couples like these, I ask them to chart how much Qualitative Time they have together in a week. It's surprising how many couples spend little or no positive, enjoyable time with one another. Often, if they can learn to spend some Qualitative Time together doing something they both like, many of their problems will clear up quite quickly. I am not suggesting that Qualitative Time is a panacea for all couple conflict, but it can be quite useful in bringing couples closer together. In summary, Qualitative Time is an essential part of any relationship, and especially a love relationship. It brings couples closer together and helps create a bond of friendship between them.

Diffused Time. While Individual Time is time spent ALONE, and Qualitative Time is time people spend TOGETHER, Diffused Time is characterized by a PARTIAL INVOLVEMENT with your mate. Diffused Time refers to giving less than your undivided attention to another person. In fact, you are usually doing two or more things simultaneously. You are often trying to meet your own needs and those of your partner at the same time. For example, you could be cooking, which you enjoy, and talking to your partner, which your mate enjoys, at the same time. You are trying, then, to meet your needs and those of your mate at the same time. Diffused Time is one of the most common ways people spend time. During Diffused Time, you can engage in more than one activity, not having to give anyone your total, undivided attention. Anyone can work on a project and simultaneously take time out to daydream about something else. What man hasn't watched a football game and also carried on an absent-minded conversation with his mate? What mother hasn't cooked dinner while listening to a child's woes at school that day?

Diffused Time, unlike Individual or Qualitative Time, may not always be positive. Interaction with your mate by means of Diffused Time may or may not be satisfactory to either or both of you. Diffused Time is satisfactory when you don't have strong needs for time alone or for the intensity of Qualitative Time.

There are times when this way of relating, however, become unsatisfactory to either you or your mate. Quite often, in a particular interaction, you may not be totally involved with or in total contact with the other person. When either of you feels a need for more complete communication, this situation can prove unsatisfactory. For instance, when a husband talks to his wife while simultaneously responding to the children, his wife can become annoyed and frustrated if she wants his complete attention just then. When either a man's or a woman's needs are not being met, that specific interaction is no longer conflict-free time.

The main characteristics of Diffused Time are:
1. A man and woman are interacting.
2. One or both partners are engaged in two or more activities simultaneously.
3. As a result, the involvement with one another is PARTIAL.
4. This partial involvement may be acceptable or unacceptable to one or both partners.

Diffused Time is one of the most common ways of spending time in a relationship. It may or may not be satisfying, depending on your needs at that time. Its main characteristic is your giving only partial attention to your mate as you do several things at once.

summary

Your main goal should be to increase the Qualitative Time and the Individual Time you spend. The result of getting good Qualitative Time with your mate is often the development of a close interpersonal relationship. Qualitative Time gives you both the chance to get to know one another better, to build your relationship in a positive, enjoyable way, and to become friends.

PART TWO

Neurotic Love Relationships

7

the self-defeating relationship

introduction

In Part I we have noted the skills couples need to make a relationship rewarding and happy. When partners are not successful in meeting their needs as a couple, they run the likelihood of developing a self-defeating and neurotic relationship.

The goal in this chapter is to explore and understand the major characteristics of the self-defeating relationship. Once a person understands the important variables of this type of relationship, he or she can employ constructive ways to change it. So let's begin by examining how the self-defeating relationship develops.

low self-esteem

When one or both partners in a relationship have not yet learned to love themselves as people, their relationship may do them more harm than good. Instead of growing as individuals and as a couple, they become constricted and unhappy in their lives.

Those who have a poor opinion of themselves generally turn to others for approval. If you love yourself, you want the love and approval of others but it is *not* a necessity for your sense of self-esteem or identity. If you really haven't yet learned to love yourself, however, you tend to believe that you *have to have* the constant approval and reassurance of others. If you don't get their approval, you don't feel right about yourself as a person. Your sense of self is threatened. What happens then is that your self-esteem rests in others' hands rather than in your own.

This lack of self-esteem has several consequences. First you become more *dependent* on others. You usually look up to them and see them as more powerful, knowledgeable, capable, adequate than yourself. You often put them on a pedestal and see them as a source of strength. The stronger you see someone else to be, however, the weaker you become. Over a period of time, this type of relationship can grow lopsided, with the overly dependent seeing themselves as less and less capable while seeing their mates grow stronger and more powerful. This perception leads the dependent mate to become ever more dependent and inadequate. Moreover, although dependent mates both love and admire their "stronger" partners, they also develop a good deal of resentment towards them because of this dependency.

A second outcome of not loving yourself is the fear of being your *real self* with people. Since you don't accept yourself, you don't think others will either. So, instead of sharing who you are, you begin to play *roles* and put on masks when dealing with the people you are close to. Often the masks are geared to pleasing others because you are constantly seeking ways to gain their approval. You are overly nice or exceptionally accommodating, trying to meet others' needs so they will like and approve of you. Other such individuals may act indifferent, as if they don't need the approval of others. Craving recognition and approval, they are nevertheless afraid to show it, sure they will be rebuffed or rejected. This strategy of playing roles and hiding true feelings, all in the attempt to gain the approval of others, almost always backfires. Not only do others end up disapproving of your behavior, but they often become angry and rejecting — exactly the reaction feared most.

These two traits then — an overreliance or dependence on a loved one and an unwillingness to be your true self — set the stage for self-defeating love relationships. In a self-defeating relationship, usually one, and most often both, partners do not feel good about themselves. In my own clinical experience, I have determined that three further characteristics recur in self-defeating relationships.

1. Couples have an unequal balance of power between them.
2. Couples lack role flexibility.
3. Couples get locked into rigid styles and patterns of interaction.

unequal balance of power

In my ten years of working with couples, I have found that the issue of control is the most critical in the formation and continuance of either a self-defeating or a healthy relationship. All couples early in their relationship must deal with the issue of who is in control, who makes the decisions. Before they get involved with each other, individuals can make their own decisions about their goals in life, their values and preferences. Once they're in a relationship, however, they have to work as a couple to make decisions. Working as a couple on the myriad problems and choices couples face raises the issue of control and power.

It will help to look at what a healthy balance of power is in a relationship before examining the problem areas. I would describe a healthy balance of power in a relationship as an equal balance of power or a 50/50 relationship. In a 50/50 relationship, both people enter the relationship feeling good about themselves and with a positive sense of self. They are each willing to give to the other person but also are able to stand up for themselves to meet their own needs. With these attitudes, couples can work in a collaborative manner. Neither person then needs to bully or be bullied by the other.

With a healthy balance of power, you respect your mate's needs as well as your own. Neither of you loses self-esteem in a 50/50 relationship. We should remember, however, that there are times in a healthy relationship when one of you does, in fact, give in to the other. When that happens it can be a respectable 60/40 split. There may come a time when you sensibly say to your loved one, "You make the decision here. You're the expert, I'm not." One partner then relinquishes power for a time to the other. At times, of course, the other will reciprocate by relinquishing power to his or her partner. In the basic healthy relationship, however, there is an overall consistent and equal sharing of power. You respect each other's rights, and neither of you is able to push the other around because you each stand up for yourself. As each of you stands up for yourself, you gain your mate's respect. You both are willing to work hand in hand to solve problems, define collective goals, and make joint decisions. Thus, neither takes advantage of the other; both work together 50/50.

Often when couples work for a 50/50 balance of power, there is more open conflict between them. This conflict is neither bad nor something to be avoided. What is more important is how this conflict is resolved. So long as conflict is resolved with respect maintained for the needs of both persons, the conflict does not damage the relationship. It is when differences are repeatedly resolved so that one mate "wins" and the other "loses" that conflict is harmful.

In the self-defeating relationship there is an unequal balance of power: what I call the 80/20 split. In this relationship, one partner has a tremendous amount of overt control over the relationship. The one who has 80% of the power makes most and sometimes all of the decisons. The one with only 20%

of the power tends to be passive, to cater to and give in to the powerful partner.

The 80/20 split can be illustrated by the case of Bob and Sue. Bob and Sue are in their mid-forties and have been marrried for twenty-two years. Bob is a very successful businessman and Sue is a housewife. They have raised two children, and in the last several years, Sue has started working part-time in the registrar's office of the local junior college.

Bob and Sue were raised in families where both sets of parents came from the old country. Both their fathers had been fairly autocratic and their mothers quiet and submissive to their husbands. Bob and Sue had followed this pattern. Bob made all the decisions in the house, and Sue went along with this arrangement. Sue stated she felt this arrangement was right because this is the way her parents did it, and she was comfortable with Bob being in charge.

Over time this relationship had become more and more lopsided, however, because increasingly Bob had taken advantage of this situation. He simply went to work and really did nothing else to support the family. Sue prepared the meals, paid the bills, did the income tax, cleaned the house. Bob tended to be totally in charge of the relationship; if he wanted something, he got it. He decided where they were to invest their money, which restaurant they went to dine at, and how they were to spend their free time. While Bob made these decisions, Sue did most of the work. On those rare occasions when he didn't get his way, he immediately shouted and screamed, and Sue almost always gave in to his threats and bullying. Periodically, Sue herself blew up — threw dishes, screamed — but afterwards she felt guilty and quickly went back to her nonassertive posture. This had been the pattern for the last twenty years. Marital therapy was initiated not by Sue but by Bob, who felt that he no longer loved his wife. He was, in fact, contemplating a separation.

There is clearly an unequal balance of power in this relationship. Bob and Sue's case shows what happens when there is an 80/20 split in power. When you have a greater share of the power (80%), over time you gradually begin to *lose respect* for your mate, given his or her unwillingness to stand up to you. As you lose respect for him or her, you stop loving your mate.

You might think that it would be the person with only 20% of the power who would want to break off such a relationship, since this person is the one whose needs are not getting met and who feels used and mistreated. Almost always, however, it is the partner who controls the relationship who is dissatisfied enough to think of terminating the relationship. When you are the person without power, normally you believe you can't live without your mate, which is one of the reasons you continuously give in to him or her. Over time you lose self-confidence in your own abilities, and then become even more dependent on your mate. The last thing you want is termination of the relationship.

When you allow your partner to control the relationship, you also build up a good deal of resentment. If you aren't aware of this anger and rage, it often manifests itself in somatic concerns such as headaches, stomach problems, asthma or stiff joints. If you are aware of your anger, you either remain passive and overcontrolled, or at times blow up and "throw things," as Sue did.

We can see in the example of Bob and Sue the two traits discussed earlier that often characterize the self-defeating relationship: Sue's dependence and her fear of being her real self played a prominent role in their marriage. When Sue learned to be less dependent and to share her honest feelings by being assertive with Bob, their relationship moved to a more equal status of 50/50.

Sometimes when individuals feel they have no power (20%) they fight back in unconscious or indirect ways. Since they feel they can't confront their loved ones directly and have an influence on them in the area of control and decision-making, they find round-about ways to get back at their more powerful mates.

Let's take another case history. Gail allowed her husband, Fred, to make all the decisions in their marriage. A particularly upsetting, but characteristic, incident occurred when Gail's husband changed their vacation plans without consulting her. He changed both the time of the month they were to go on a holiday (which was an inconvenience for her schedule), and also invited two other couples to join them, although they had originally planned to get away by themselves for a second honeymoon. In addition, Gail didn't get along well with the other couples, which was a further source of irritation. Gail's husband made a unilateral decision about the change in vacation plans, simply informing her of it on his way to work one morning. She said nothing about it although she was upset.

Later that week, at a dinner party in which Fred was entertaining important business clients, Gail made some rather inappropriate comments to his clients, embarrasssing Fred in front of his associates. At the time she was unaware of the connection between her "spoiled" vacation and her indirect expression of anger at her husband by publicly embarrassing him. Later on, as she discussed this incident in therapy, she was able to see the connection between her acquiescence to her husband's demands and her "paying him back" later.

In situations like this one with Gail and Fed, Fred had 80% of the power and control of the relationship. Gail turned the tables, however, and gained 80% of the power by getting even with Fred in an indirect manner. It's important to remember that when individuals feel they have no power, sometimes they fight back in unconscious and/or passive-aggressive ways, thus ending up with 80% of the power in another respect. That is, they withhold goods and services that they know their spouses want. Two things commonly withheld when the balance of power is uneven are sex and emotional support. In this case, Gail withheld being the nice, polite, socially gracious wife when Fred needed it. She thus temporarily gained control of the relationship. We could diagram this process as follows:

80/20 split — Overt Control (Fred wins)
20/80 split — Covert Control (Gail wins)

This issue of control and decision-making is critical in all relationships. Trouble ensues when the balance of power becomes lopsided and unequal. Usually both partners are unhappy with an 80/20 split of power. Quite often both partners are struggling with dependency conflicts and low self-esteem. If you are the person with control of the relationship, your own dependency needs are often *hidden*. You feel good about yourself on the surface because you are "in charge" of the relationship. But your sense of security and self-esteem could be threatened if you lost your mate (i.e., in separation or divorce) or had to operate on a more equal basis. I have counseled many people who stated how easily they could live without their "weaker" mates, only to find upon separation how dependent they themselves really were. When you are the person with only 20% of the power, you usually are more aware of the tendency to cling and be dependent on your mate. You are also aware that your self-esteem seems somehow attached to your mate's approving of and liking you. Whatever the case, an unequal balance of power creates real problems in a relationship.

Up to this point we have discussed basically two types of relationships: a healthy 50/50 relationship that has equal give-and-take between partners; and a self-defeating, unequal relationship where one mate has more power and control that the other. A third option is an open power struggle between partners, in which neither compromises or gives an inch, but both fight it out for control. Such a battle for control almost always ends in stalemate. As a general rule, these power struggles usually lead to a termination of the relationship or to one of the two options we have already explored.

role flexibility versus role rigidity

In addition to dealing with the issue of power and control, couples need to deal with how they are going to interact with one another on a day-to-day basis. All individuals interact with their partners in different roles. The healthy couple can utilize a number of roles. One of the things that happens when people have not developed positive self-esteem or a positive and clear-cut sense of identity, is that they begin to develop rigid roles which they play with their mates. Therefore, the self-defeating couple often has just one role in which they interact with one another.

Responding in a healthy manner to a mate requires what I refer to as role flexibility. That is, partners can choose different roles from which to interact that meet their own needs as well as the needs of their loved ones in a given situation. There are three major roles, or psychological ego states as Eric Berne referred to them, that everyone possesses. These three roles are: Adult, Parent and Child. In the Adult role, you make decisions, set goals, and find solutions to problems; in your role as Parent, you nurture and support your partner; and finally, as a Child, you play with and enjoy one another.

The healthy couple has the flexibility to assume all three major roles. Let's examine this in more detail. For example, there are times when couples need to act as Adults with one another. They may need to make Adult decisions together on how they are going to invest their money, how they are going to raise their children, what they're going to do in terms of career goals, how they spend their leisure time. Both need to be able to utilize adult problem-solving skills so they can take care of themselves. Only one may play the Adult role, but if the relationship is to be really successful, both have to play the Adult role.

Both partners should also be able to be effective Parents to one another. When you Parent your mate, you lend a helping hand when the one you love is down or has a personal problem. For example, if a man has just had a particularly rough week with business problems, his wife can be a Parent to him, nurture him, and meet his emotional needs with support and reassurance. At times, these roles will be reversed. The wife who is burdened with young children all day can be parented by her husband, who takes the time to listen to her, to tell her he cares, and to take her out to dinner for a much-needed break.

Finally, it is important in a relationship that you sometimes be a Child, allowing yourself to be spontaneous, fun-loving, and playful. The role of Child allows you to enjoy yourself and play with your mate. Such play can range from laughing and joking over a game of cards to going for a bike ride to just playfully teasing one another. Couples need to engage in fun and enjoyable activities.

The ability to play these three major roles enables you to meet your needs, build your self-esteem, meet the needs of your mate, and deal with problems as they arise. Role flexibility means that you are able to act in ways that will be effective, whatever a specific situation calls for. If your partner needs you to provide support, you can be the helpful Parent. If your mate needs help in making Adult decisions on some problem, you can participate as an Adult. And finally, you can be a Child and meet the needs of your loved one for fun and play. When the situation warrants, you and your mate will reverse roles and he or she will do these things for you. Clearly, couples need the ability to play different roles to fit various situations.

In self-defeating relationships couples develop role rigidity; that is, they utilize only one, sometimes two, of the three roles just described. Instead of having the ability to move from role to role (i.e., Parent to Adult to Child, and back to Adult) as the situation demands, these couples get locked into acting in one role most of the time in their relationship with their mates. This one role becomes overdeveloped in their lives. For example, you may tend always to Parent or always to act like an Adult. When you utilize only one role, it is difficult to meet either your own or your partner's needs consistently. This role rigidity often comes about because of fear of being your real self with your mate. You choose instead to play a circumscribed role that feels safe and secure.

For example, Guy was a computer programmer who excelled at his job because of his Adult problem-solving skills and logical mind. The Adult skills gained him high respect at the office and also helped him at home with his wife, Betty, when it came to such things as planning a budget, analyzing investment opportunities, and deciding how best to budget their time so that they could both work and do household chores. Guy's intellectual skills and rational mind were great at problem-solving tasks because he always weighed all the possibilities and then made good objective decisions. In short, Guy operated like an efficient computer.

Guy's Adult skills, however, didn't help when his wife had a rough day and needed some special attention and comforting. Nor did his Adult skills help when his wife wanted just to relax and have a good time. Guy found it difficult to be a nurturing Parent to Betty and meet her emotional needs, and he found it equally hard to relax, let his hair down and enjoy himself as a Child. Guy constantly related to Betty and others as a super-rational Adult because he simply had not learned how to be a helpful, nurturing Parent or a playful, fun-loving Child. Guy's behavior put a great strain on their marriage because it narrowed the scope of what they could do and limited the degree to which Guy could meet Betty's needs, as well as his own.

Being an overdeveloped Adult like Guy, with limited facility to be the nurturing Parent or playful Child, is an example of role rigidity. To be so limited stifles personal growth and constricts the relationship. Guy played this role because all his life he had been reinforced only for his intellectual abilities. He had been the "egghead" type in school, and though he felt secure with his exceptional scholastic abilities, he was lacking in social skills, athletic interests, and the ability to relax and have a good time. Guy had to learn other ways of relating to people — which he found frightening at first — before he could relax and give up his constant role as the super-rational Adult.

Let's illustrate this process with another example. Debbie had grown up in a home in which her father had numerous physical and psychological problems. Being the only child, she was pressed into service with her mother to attend to her father's various complaints. The parents were divorced when Debbie was sixteen, at which time her father was awarded custody of her and she then took over sole responsibility for his care. She took him to Alcoholics Anonymous meetings for his alcoholism, made sure he got to work on time, cooked for him, did all his laundry. Over the next four or five years, she became a most overprotective Parent to her father. Her father's guilt-inducing ways drove her to continue Parenting him. Finally, Debbie broke away from home by moving to another city. She still kept in constant telephone contact with her father, however, and was ever reassuring him and listening to his various problems.

Debbie got married a year later, as much to escape her father as to be with Frank, her new husband. Though she thought her problems were over, within six months she was Parenting her husband as much as she had her father. She did everything for him: offered unsolicited advice on his business concerns, did all the housework, and was overprotective and solicitous with any problem he had. Within a short time she drove her husband away. He stated he felt he had in Debbie an overcontrolling mother, not a wife. It's easy to see that Debbie was quite adroit at using her Parenting skills but spent very little time being Adult or playful Child. The overdevelopment of her Parent role left Debbie little freedom to be with her husband, nor did it add much personal enjoyment to her own life. Debbie had to learn to stop inappropriately Parenting her husband as she had done to her father. In addition, she had to develop more of her Child skills and to relax and be more playful in her life. She also had to use Adult skills to be more an equal partner in her marriage than a Parent.

Again, it is important to emphasize that *all* individuals need to relate to their loved ones in all three roles — as Parent, Adult, and Child. If they overemphasize one of these roles, they constrict themselves and hamper the flexibility of their relationship.

self-defeating styles

In the previous section we examined how rigid role-playing can lead to an overemphasis of one aspect of an individual's personality to the exclusion of other positive attributes. Now we'll see how couples with rigid roles often form complementary role patterns with one another.

Such couples tend to play one of three roles in their relationship. First is the Passive role, in which you let your mate take charge of the relationship. Some common passive roles are the Nice Guy who is always willing to go along and do the right thing, who doesn't want to make waves or offend anyone. Then there is the Helpless Child, who feels useless and inadequate and therefore needs a "stronger" partner to take over. There is also the Dummy, who feels intellectually inadequate to cope successfully in this world. Finally, there is the Self-Effacing or Appeasing individual, who is constantly giving in and letting the other control the relationship.

The second type of role is that of the Helper, taking care of and protecting the mate. A common helper role is the Intellectual Know-It-All. When you play this role, you use your intellectual abilities to control and dominate a mate. You always have the right answer and know how a problem should be solved. Next is the Overprotective Parent. If you fall into this role, you constantly want to help and do everything for your partner.

The third type of role often assumed is the Attacker. Employing this technique you attack and criticize your loved one a great deal. Some common attacking roles are the Critical Parent role, in which you are always nagging and telling your mate how to do everything. You treat your partner like a child. Another attacking role is the Angry Mate, who is always mad and upset over everything, constantly bitching and yelling.

So there are three major roles people in self-defeating relationships can play: Helper, Passive, and Attacker. What happens most often in the self-defeating relationship is a complementary match-up between two of these styles. For example, an Overprotective mate matches with a Helpless Child, or an Intellectual Know-It-All matches up with a Dummy. They complement one another but, as we shall see, to the detriment of both. Let's examine some of the most common self-defeating match-up roles couples can play.

angry mate versus appeasing mate

In this type of relationship, one partner is chronically angry. The other is an Appeasing Mate who not only accepts this anger as if it were justified, but continually tries to please and placate the angry partner. The Angry Mate almost always controls the relationship (80% of the power) while the Appeasing Mate is compliant and gives in to the more demanding partner. Over a period of time, the two become locked into this pattern so that the relationship is governed by it. The Angry Mate can and does get upset over any little thing, and the Appeasing Mate attempts to placate him or her, no matter how unreasonable the demands.

Let's illustrate this type of relationship with the case of Ralph and Linda. Ralph is in his mid-twenties and works in a lumberyard as a cashier and handyman. His wife, Linda, is a high school teacher. Early in their marriage Ralph had planned to become a doctor, but had continually postponed applying to medical schools for fear he would be turned down. His present job was below what he was capable of doing with a college degree and he seemed to lack incentive to advance his career at the lumberyard. His wife was understanding at first, but gradually grew more and more resentful of Ralph's not making anything of himself.

Ralph, too, seemed discouraged and frustrated in his life. He was unhappy in his job but didn't know how to change it. Over a period of several years he withdrew more from people and he and Linda socialized less. Ralph no longer played racquetball and tennis as he had in the past. Linda said it was difficult to get Ralph to help with the household chores, be with friends, or just go out to dinner. Meanwhile, Linda's job as a teacher was rewarding. She had developed some close friendships at work and had joined a health studio and had lost twenty-five pounds. Over a period of time, Linda became more self-confident and successful, and began to become more resentful of Ralph's doing little or nothing with his life. Linda expressed her anger more openly to Ralph now. At first, Ralph defended himself and fought back, but as he doubted his own abilities more and more, he began to acquiesce to Linda's angry outbursts. Within a year and a half, the pattern of Linda being the Angry Mate and Ralph the Appeasing Mate had been set.

At first, Linda was angry at Ralph for legitimate reasons — his not helping with household chores, avoiding a career decision, not working harder on his job, avoiding friends. As Ralph placated her and attempted to soothe her anger with promises to do better and apologies and excuses, however, she only grew more resentful. Soon Linda was angry at Ralph over next to nothing, stating, "I don't like the way Ralph eats or combs his hair." She admitted, "This is crazy, I know I shouldn't be angry at him for these things. What's wrong with me?" The more Ralph appeased Linda, the angrier she got. Let's see why this happens.

To begin with, Ralph, the Appeasing Mate, didn't feel good about himself, being frustrated primarily in the area of his achievement needs. He was afraid either to apply to medical school or to seek advancement at his present job. His seeming paralysis in the area of career led to a real loss of self-confidence and affected his other needs. He began to lose confidence in and respect for himself, and finally felt like he was a "nobody." As he grew more depressed, he began avoiding people and spent more and more time simply watching television. Because Ralph was totally down on himself and saw his life as going nowhere, he gave up more and more of his control in the marriage relationship. It went from 50/50 to 80/20.

In addition, he began to be more of a Helpless Child in the relationship. He began to believe that he couldn't live without his wife. This behavior led to his "smothering" his wife, always wanting to be with her, and to his accepting an appeasing stance because he was fearful that if he were assertive with her he would lose her. The more appeasing Ralph became, however, the less Linda wanted to be with him. She now saw Ralph as weak and dependent on her, and began to lose her respect for him. Much of her unreasonable anger was an attempt to provoke Ralph into standing up for himself so that she could respect and love him again. At this point, however, Ralph was intimidated by her anger and afraid to assert himself for fear of losing her, and so became even more appeasing. As a result, this pattern became dominant in their interactions and they grew further and further apart.

They sought counseling when Linda decided she should terminate the marriage, even though she felt she still loved Ralph. In therapy, Ralph learned to come to terms with his achievement conflicts. He gave up the idea of medical school and decided to seek advancement in his present job. Gradually his confidence grew, and he began to be more assertive with Linda and less the Appeasing Mate. As he grew more assertive, Linda respected him more. She found herself being less angry over petty things, and their relationship became a more balanced 50/50 arrangement. Though in this case, Ralph and Linda's marital problems had a positive outcome, in many cases such problem relationships end in separation or divorce.

overprotective mate versus helpless-child mate

In this second type of relationship, the dominant mate (i.e., the one who controls 80% of the power) does not use anger and aggression but rather a sense of overprotectiveness and overindulgence to gain control. In such a relationship we have the Overprotective Mate doing many things that his or her partner could easily learn to do. The other person becomes the Helpless Child who cannot do anything without the "stronger" mate's support and approval. In this type of relationship, the Helpless Child mate feels inadequate personally and often professionally, not feeling up to the demands of being an adult. Such people are often underachievers and tend to turn to their more adequate mates for protection and assistance. Overprotective Mates enjoy playing Parent. They generally derive good feelings about themselves from being able to help and nurture their less adequate partners. Sometimes they feel they were cast into the role of Parent because their loved ones feel helpless and inadequate, and in fact, give them no choice but to play the role of Parent.

Let's use another case to illustrate this type of relationship. Bill is in his early thirties and supervises a computer program terminal for a large company. Lois, who is in her late twenties, has an advanced degree in marketing but has never worked in her professional field. Since graduate school she has worked for a department store doing minimum-wage work. They have been married for five years. In their marriage Bill makes most of the major decisions. He decides how they will invest their money, where they will go on vacation, what new addition needs to be made to the house. Lois has not only accepted Bill's decisions in such matters but has indeed welcomed them. She states she doesn't know what she'd do without Bill because he is so resourceful and knowledgeable.

Examining his past, we find Bill grew up in a large family. He was the oldest of five children. The father deserted the home when Bill was twelve, and in many ways Bill became the head of the household at that time, assuming many of his father's responsibilities. When Bill was sixteen, his mother was hospitalized for a heart condition for several months, and Bill took on even more responsibilities in the family. He took care of his younger brothers and sisters, as well as looking after his mother when she returned home. By the time Bill was seventeen he was the parent of the household, taking care of everyone. Bill felt comfortable in this role and was constantly reinforced by his mother for the good job he was doing. Bill was very responsible, doing odd jobs throughout high school and putting himself through college with part-time work. After college, Bill rose quickly in the company he joined, becoming a supervisor in his mid-twenties, and by age thirty he was one of the youngest managers in the firm. Bill made a good salary and was able to help his younger brothers and sisters with financial assistance so that they could attend college. At the time they came for counseling, Bill was even helping one of Lois' brothers with financial support through college.

Lois was the youngest of three children in her family, raised by overprotective and overindulgent parents. Lois remembers having no chores or responsibilities while she was growing up. She remembers her mother picking out her clothes for her, not only as a child but even when Lois was in high school. Lois never learned to cook because her mother insisted that she do it instead. Lois remembers her parents as being very loving but also allowing her little personal freedom. Lois stated she doesn't remember wanting for anything as a child. She always did well in school, which pleased her parents. Other than the expectation that she get good grades (which she did with ease), Lois' parents placed no other demands on her. Lois did well in college and graduated with honors. She met Bill a year before she graduated and married him right after graduation. At that time, Bill was an up-and-coming young executive, already quite successful in his job.

Lois did not work for the first two years of their marriage but stayed home, taking a painting class or two. She decided she didn't want to use her marketing degree and eventually got a job in a small department store, with little responsibility. During this time, Lois decided to become an artist. To this end, she took art classes at the university and in the community. But she pursued her interest in art no further than taking courses. She stated that she had plans to become a professional painter but didn't feel qualified to do so at present.

In this marriage, we see that the wife is playing Helpless Child, having never grown up. Both her parents and now her husband indulge her and expect little or no responsible behavior from her. She complies in turn, feeling inadequate and helpless to change this pattern.

Lois initiated therapy, saying, in an individual session, that she was not sure if she loved her husband because he seemed "so straight, so establishment, so much like my parents." She had recently become enamoured of a man several years her junior with whom she worked, who seemed like a "free spirit" and far more adventurous than her staid and solid husband. This young man would work for several months, then quit his job to travel and work on a steamer for several months. He espoused the use of drugs and free love, and to Lois he appeared to be "grown up," because he was, as she said, "his own man." Lois was comtemplating being "grown up" also by leaving her husband and traveling and working as she pleased.

In an individual session, Bill stated that recently he had begun to feel that his wife was not carrying her share in the relationship. He felt she could get a better-paying job and help out with the expenses, or that she should become an artist and quit just taking classes. In the last several months, Bill had been putting more pressure on his wife to change in this direction, which had created considerable strain in their relationship.

After a number of months in therapy, Lois learned that growing up was more difficult than just being adventurous and free-spirited. For Lois, it meant learning to make more of her own decisions and becoming less dependent on her husband. A big step for her was working on her achievement needs. In this case, she decided to become an artist. She stopped taking classes and began to show her art work at local art exhibits. Over the course of a year this led to her winning several awards and finally selling her first pictures.

Bill also had to change, for he was secure in the role of protective parent. It was something he had done most of his life. He had to allow his wife to grow up and become more independent of him. At first this caused him some anxiety, but as time went on, he realized he had more freedom since he didn't always have to take care of his wife. These changes allowed both Bill and Lois to grow closer as Adults.

In the relationship of the Overprotective Mate and the Helpless-Child Mate, the Helpless Mate has to learn to grow up and become a more independent person. Such people need to work on fulfilling their needs for identity and usually their achievement needs as well. Overprotective Mates must change also. They need to learn to let go and let their partners grow and develop as individuals in their own right. The Overprotective Mate is also often an all-work and no-play person, as was the case with Bill. He rarely took time off for himself to engage in leisure-time activities because he was so busy working or taking care of the needs of others. Part of Bill's therapy was learning to relax, meet his needs for fun and play and be more of a Child. Both spouses needed to make some major changes for this marriage to become successful.

nagging-parent mate versus irresponsible-child mate

In this third type of relationship we have the Nagging-Parent Mate who is constantly annoyed with and critical of the other person, and an Irresponsible Child who won't grow up.

In this relationship, the dominant partner is not, as you would imagine, the one who plays Nagging Parent. Rather, it is the Irresponsible-Child Mate who is most often in control of the relationship. People who play the Irresponsible Child tend to do what they want when they want. They don't worry much about the consequences of their behavior, at least at the time they are engaging in that behavior. Irresponsible Mates tend to be self-centered and self-interest-oriented. They like to pursue their own interests regardless of how it intereferes with the rights or needs of others. They can have trouble meeting deadlines, holding onto a job, being prompt, or sensing and meeting someone else's needs. They can often be charming and gracious, but such charm wears thin after a while, especially if you have to live with them.

It is unusual for Nagging Mates to start off being bitchy and nagging. Rather, usually they have been submissive and passive with their more irresponsible partners. They think and hope their loved ones will "shape up" in time. They expect their mates eventually to act in the same adult, responsible manner as they themselves do. When this doesn't happen, they are confused and hurt. They think their irresponsible partners just need to "learn how to act." They try using logic or giving calm, rational lectures on why one should get to work on time or not tell off-color jokes at the boss' cocktail party. When they find that their mate doesn't heed their advice and practical solutions, they grow angry and hurt. Less logical arguments and more nagging often follow. Over time Nagging Parent Mates become exasperated and defeated, since all their good advice seems to fall on deaf ears. Their nagging behavior then is a reaction to the partner's irresponsible behavior. Over time each person's behavior becomes more exaggerated. The Irresponsible Mate becomes more irresponsible and the Nagging Mate bitches and nags more. Both partners tend to develop a good deal of resentment and hurt feelings.

Let's use the case of Bonnie and Phil to illustrate this type of self-defeating relationship problem. Bonnie and Phil are both in their late twenties and have been married for seven years. They have no children. Bonnie works as a buyer for a large department store. Phil works as a salesman. Bonnie is the oldest of three children. She grew up in a home in which her parents were "semi-strict." She remembers all the children had chores to do and that she was given the most responsibility because she was the oldest. She was close to her parents and described her family as a loving one. Bonnie graduated from high school with honors, got a college degree in management, and became a buyer in a department store. She met Phil while in her last year of college and married him shortly after she graduated.

Phil was the youngest of three children. He grew up being the baby of the family and unquestionably was badly spoiled. He stated he generally got what he wanted. He could talk his parents — especially his mother — into getting him whatever he desired. Discipline was quite lax in Phil's household, and all the children were given lots of freedom to do as they pleased. Phil did average work in high school because he didn't feel "motivated," and spent most of his time engaged in sports, playing basketball and baseball. Phil spent two years in college but dropped out because he didn't like school: "It was too much work." Phil became a salesman because he liked people and enjoyed doing something different every day. In six years, Phil had five different jobs. Phil's bosses always felt he did excellent work when motivated, but otherwise just coasted and did only enough to get by. Phil had quit several jobs just before he was asked to resign from his current position. He claimed that he got bored and wanted more money and excitement. Phil has a charming personality and makes a good first impression, and so has had no trouble in getting jobs. Two of Phil's job moves in the past, however, had required him to move to another city. Each time Bonnie had quit a successful job to move with Phil.

In the first year of this marriage, both felt close to one another. Bonnie described Phil as helpful with household chores and considerate of her needs. Phil saw Bonnie as supportive and affectionate. Over time, however, Phil became more and more self-centered. He rarely did any housework unless nagged constantly about it. He spent all his free time playing baseball with the boys and rarely wanted to do anything with Bonnie. As a salesman he set his own hours and often took one or two days off, when he went to the beach or shopping. Since they had a joint checking account, Phil "borrowed" from Bonnie's share if he had spent his own share. The result was that Bonnie's money was used to pay all the bills while Phil's money went for his own personal use.

For a long time, Bonnie was passive and submissive in the face of Phil's growing irresponsible behavior. She simply hoped Phil would change and become more responsible. Her resentment grew, however, as his behavior became less and less responsible and she began to bitch and nag at Phil to stay home, not play ball with the boys, and help with the housework. At times her "nagging" worked, and Phil reluctantly stayed and helped out. More often, though, Phil said he'd "do it later" and took off. As this pattern continued, Bonnie and Phil grew further and further apart. Phil began to see Bonnie as a critical parent trying to constrict his freedom, something no one had ever done before. Phil felt he no longer loved and cared for Bonnie. Bonnie in turn was losing her love for Phil. She saw him as irresponsible, unaffectionate and unwilling to change and "grow up." Eventually Phil and Bonnie separated and later got a divorce. Their differences were simply too great to be overcome.

summary

Up to this point we have examined some of the consequences of not loving yourself and/or not having met one or more of the areas couples need to address successfully as discussed in previous chapters. If people have not met these prerequisites, they tend to form self-defeating relationships. In these relationships they are looking for their partner to give the love and approval they haven't yet given themselves. Not loving themselves, they often don't reveal their real selves to their partners. The results can be an unequal balance of power, limited ways of interacting with one another, and, finally, neurotic interactional patterns or styles. We have also looked at three of the most common of these self-defeating interactional styles: The Angry vs. Appeasing Partner, the Over-Protective vs. Helpless Partner, and the Nagging vs. Irresponsible Partner.

Since self-defeating relationships hinder our individual growth and cripple relationships, we shall next examine what specific steps are needed to correct this type of relationship.

8

treating the self-defeating relationship

introduction

In the last chapter we explored some of the major elements of the self-defeating love relationship. In this chapter our goal will be to understand specifically what can be done to change these types of interactions between men and women to produce healthier and happier relationships.

We will reexamine the three most common self-defeating relationships (Angry Mate vs. Appeasing Mate; Overprotective Mate vs. Helpless-Child Mate; and Nagging-Parent Mate vs. Irresponsible-Child Mate), and outline ways to treat each problem relationship.

angry mate versus the appeasing mate

In this relationship, one partner uses anger to control the relationship. Often the Angry Partner reports getting angry over just about everything his or her mate does. The Appeasing Mate, on the other hand, is a peacemaker: "Peace at Any Price" becomes his or her motto. Appeasing Mates usually feel overly dependent and needful of their loved ones. They are afraid of offending their mates or, more fundamentally, of losing their mates' affection. Consequently, they usually give in to the Angry Mate's demands, whether reasonable or unreasonable. Generally, this approach boomerangs, and their Angry Mates become more distant and cold, even though they have gotten what they want. Appeasement doesn't really satisfy the Angry Partner. It often seems that Angry Mates are really hoping their more passive partners will stand up to them and say "no" more often. These Angry Partners often equate respect with being assertive, and when their Appeasing Mates give in, Angry Partners lose first respect and then love for them.

Let's look at the case of Fred and Cathy and what needs to be done to help this type of couple. Fred is a successful real estate broker, well-respected in the community. He serves on a number of boards and has been president of several local civic organizations. Although Fred is financially stable now, he grew up in a very poor environment. He was the youngest of four children, raised by his mother because his father had died two years after Fred was born. Fred's mother never remarried; on her own, she worked hard to raise Fred and his brother and sisters. Times were hard for the family. His mother was a fairly critical woman who pushed all her children to achieve and be successful. Fred worked hard as a youngster, both at part-time jobs and at school; he never had time for sports, extracurricular activities, or dating. He was an excellent student and received academic honors in both high school and college. While in college he met Cathy and they got married. After college, Fred went into real estate, putting in eighteen-hour days in the drive to become "successful." By age forty he was financially secure and could have retired had he so desired.

Cathy was the older of two girls in her family. Her younger sister had had numerous physical problems through the years; as a result she was pampered and coddled by their mother. Cathy remembers doing almost all of the chores and housework, and, although working very hard to please her mother, never being really successful in gaining her mother's favor. Cathy's sister was the apple of her mother's eye, while Cathy took the brunt of her mother's criticism and caustic remarks. Though she was unable to please her mother, she enjoyed a warm, supportive relationship with her father.

Cathy was popular in high school, got good grades, was a cheerleader, was in the school band and glee club, and dated a great deal. After high school, Cathy worked for a local department store for two years, both selling and modeling clothes. She met Fred on a blind date. Though their courtship and the first few years of their marriage were enjoyable, Cathy found that after their first child was born Fred spent more and more time putting in long hours on his career. Over the years, Fred had little time for Cathy. He met few of her emotional needs, being much more preoccupied with "financial success" and "security." Cathy went out of her way to please and accommodate Fred. She cared for the children on her own, cooked all the meals, took care of the house. In many ways she treated Fred like royalty. She ironed all of his clothes, arranged them in his drawers, drew his bath every night, and was constantly at his beck and call. At first, Cathy enjoyed doing all these things for Fred, but he rarely reciprocated by meeting her needs for such things as dinner out or a vacation. His explanation was that they couldn't afford these things, though they were by now quite well off financially.

When Cathy stated she wanted something, Fred at once became angry and blew up at her. His reaction frightened Cathy so that she quickly backed down, and Fred almost always got his way. Over the years, Cathy gave up many of her friends because Fred did not have time to socialize. She stopped being an active member of clubs and organizations, instead devoting most of her time to raising the children and taking care of Fred. As Cathy's life became more sequestered and constricted, she became more appeasing and accommodating to Fred. During this time, she developed a number of physical problems: colitis, backaches, allergies.

Finally, when Fred felt he was no longer attracted to or in love with his wife, he and Cathy separated for a few months. When Cathy then filed for divorce, the couple sought treatment as a last chance to save their marriage. In therapy, Cathy learned that she couldn't achieve the love and close emotional relationship she desired by appeasing Fred and giving in to every demand he made. In fact, the opposite was occurring. Fred simply took her for granted and met none of Cathy's needs. If Cathy protested, usually in placating, apologetic manner, Fred simply erupted angrily and she backed down. In therapy, Cathy also learned that she had a lot of anger and resentment towards Fred. Being angry and feeling hostile had not been part of her self-image. Over time, however, Cathy realized it was not wrong to feel angry or to act assertively towards Fred. At first, Cathy was very hesitant and tentative about setting limits and being assertive with her husband. Contrary to her expectations, Fred did not exhibit such angry outbursts as he had in the past; nor did he leave her as she had feared he would. Instead, he began to show more respect for her and to meet some of her needs.

As Cathy became more assertive and stood up for her rights with her husband, many of her physical problems became less severe or vanished altogether. Cathy's assertiveness also gave her more self-confidence. She realized that in an attempt to meet all of Fred's needs over the years she had done little to met her own, especially her achievement needs. She thus took a part-time job in a publishing company, wanting to do something on her own away from the house. Her new job helped to enhance her self-esteem and confidence in herself. As Cathy became more assertive with her husband and more independent and self-confident, she became more attractive to Fred. Fred now found that he respected and cared more for Cathy. The feelings of love he thought had disappeared were now returning.

As Cathy became more assertive and demanded that some of her needs be met, Fred learned that he would have to give more on an emotional level. Fred was comfortable in the area of achievement, but learning to take time off to go out to dinner or take a two-day vacation, for example, was new for him. At first he felt uncomfortable and "unproductive" taking such breaks, but gradually he learned to enjoy himself more. His capacity to give to Cathy increased as her assertiveness towards him grew. As a result, he stopped his angry outbursts and she stopped constantly appeasing him.

We can see that in the case of Angry vs. Appeasing Mates a first step is to help Appeasing Partners become aware of their anger, accept it, and then learn to be assertive with that anger. When Appeasing Partners are able to do so, it helps them feel better about themselves and gives them more self-respect. It also allows them to have more control over their own lives and more influence in their relationship with their partners. Moreover, as a result of Appeasing Mates' becoming more assertive, Angry Mates stop having hostile temper outbursts, since such outbursts are no longer effective. As a result, Angry Mates begin to act more rationally. Also, the Angry Mates begin to respect and then love their mates more because they are standing up for themselves. Angry Mates can then learn to give more to their partners and to stop taking their loved ones for granted. The relationship becomes more balanced, less 80/20 and more 50/50.

A final change that often takes place with the Angry Mate and the Appeasing Mate occurs in the Appeasing Mate's personal life. Appeasing partners often find that over the years they have spent so much time and effort meeting their mates' needs that they have taken little time to develop and grow in their own lives, especially in the areas of achievement. They often need to do a personal assessment of their own career goals and what they would like to do with their lives. As they grow as individuals in their own rights, they not only feel better and more self-confident, but they begin to enjoy a closer relationship with their mates as well.

overprotective mate versus helpless-child mate

As we recall, this is a relationship in which one partner tends to parent and overprotect or control the other, all in his or her "best interest," deriving in fact a sense of personal satisfaction from taking care of the less competent mate. The Helpless-Child Mate has not yet developed self-confidence and needs the more successful mate to lean on. As a result, the Helpless-Child idolizes and at the same time resents the more powerful partner.

Let's illustrate this type of relationship with the case of William and Sue. William is twenty-nine, Sue twenty-four. William is a successful young architect. He met Sue three years ago when she went to work in his office as his secretary. They dated for six months and were then married. William comes from an upper-middle-class family. His father was a successful businessman. His mother raised three boys, of whom William was the oldest. The family was not very close emotionally, but much emphasis was placed on academic achievement. William excelled in high school, college, and architecture school. For him, being a successful architect was one of the most important facets of his life.

Sue was raised in an overly-indulgent, overprotective environment. She was the youngest of three girls. Her parents coddled and protected her a good deal. In high school Sue was very attractive, a cheerleader, and an average student. She developed no real talents of her own. She never attended college because she felt she was not bright enough to do so. She attended secretarial school instead, later becoming an office secretary. Because of her stunning good looks, Sue had to do little to attract men. Although she had many boyfriends in high school, however, she felt she was not "special" and that she had little to offer a man.

After high school, Sue moved into an apartment with her older sister. Shortly thereafter, she met Dan, a successful businessman about ten years her senior. Dan was quite charming and self-assured, and after she dated him for two months she impulsively married him. Problems developed almost immediately in the marriage. Dan was verbally abusive at first, later becoming physically abusive as well. In the beginning, Sue felt his abusive behavior was her fault; she blamed herself and tried harder to please Dan. Her plan backfired and, over the course of a year and a half, Dan sexually and physically abused her. Finally, in desperation, Sue told her parents about the situation; with their help and encouragement she left Dan and sought a divorce. After leaving Dan, she moved back home with her parents for a year. During that time, Sue felt protected by her parents but also under their thumb. They tended to worry constantly about her and wanted to know everything that was going on in her life. Sue did not date again until she met William some six months after her divorce.

In her mind, William was not charming or outgoing like Dan, but quiet and reserved. He was not boisterous, like Dan, but intellectual and sedate. William had an air of confidence about himself, however, that Sue admired. He knew where he was going and was successful as an architect. At this time in her life, Sue felt fragile and vulnerable; to her William seemed strong and capable. As for William, he saw Sue as gorgeous and unlike any other girl he had dated. He was surprised that she was attracted to him, for he was not athletic or particularly handsome. He realized Sue needed support and nurturing, and when they first dated he spent hours listening and talking to her. A pattern was quickly established in their relationship: Sue was weak and vulnerable, and William was strong and competent and would look after her.

After a courtship of six months, they were married. By that time the pattern of Overprotective Parent and Helpless Child was already firmly established. After several years of marriage, however, Sue's self-confidence began to grow. She had always wanted to attend college but had never thought she was bright enough to do so. With William's support and her new-found confidence, she enrolled at the local university. At first, William was encouraging. As he saw Sue achieve some academic success and become more independent, though, he began to worry that she might not need him as much as she had and he would lose his beautiful wife. William wasn't totally aware that as Sue became more independent he grew even more overprotective and overcontrolling. He would point out to Sue that she was not as intelligent as he was, calling attention to the fact that she was having difficulty in this or that course. At one point he went so far as to suggest that perhaps she should drop out of college and go back to secretarial work.

As William put more pressure on her to drop out of school, Sue began to feel trapped. She wanted to please her husband and not alienate him, but she also wanted a college education for the sense of achievement and accomplishment that it provided. Over time, a subtle tension grew between them. Over a four to five month period, Sue lost a significant amount of weight, dropping from 125 to 89 pounds. As a result of her weight loss, Sue and William argued less about school and focused more on how she could gain back her lost weight. During this time, William grew less critical and became more concerned and protective, as he had been in the past. He was totally supportive of any attempts Sue made to gain weight, but she had no appetite and nothing she did seemed to help. Sue was puzzled and upset by her excessive weight loss; it was at this point that she sought treatment.

In the course of individual and couple treatment, William and Sue changed their pattern of Overprotective Parent and Helpless Child. Sue learned that she had never really stood on her own two feet and achieved her own identity. She had always been overly-reliant and dependent on someone: her parents, her first husband, and now William. She felt she needed William; she looked up to him because of his professional success and intellectual abilities, but she also resented being so dependent on him.

She had not worked through and fully developed either her needs to be her own person or her achievement and career needs. A turning point for Sue occurred when she decided to move away from their home, by herself, to attend another college five hundred miles away. She went ostensibly because the distant college had an academic major not carried at the local university. But Sue needed to be on her own for the first time in her life. She had never

96

lived alone before, and this move symbolized growing up and becoming an adult in her own right. Sue reported that she started to gain weight almost immediately after moving to the new school; within six months she was back to her normal weight. During that year Sue enjoyed considerable academic success and she became more self-reliant and self-confident.

William was unhappy with Sue's decision to move away for a year. They took turns commuting back and forth every other weekend, however, and at the end of the year, Sue was able to move back home. She was now a person in her own right and an equal to her husband, something she had not been when they got married.

William had to change too to make this marriage survive. Since he had been playing the role of Overprotective Parent, he had to learn to let Sue go out on her own, which was hard for him to do. Although William had great confidence in his professional and intellectual abilities, he was not so confident in himself as a person. He worried that Sue would leave him once she had "seen the world" and had been on her own. William's overprotectiveness, though, had been stifling Sue and had driven her away. His ability to let go and let her move away actually brought them closer together. He found that as Sue gained independence and confidence in herself, she still loved him — but as a person, not as a parent. This put their marriage on a more equal footing. Though it was a difficult transition period, the positive gains for both far outweighed the difficult times.

We see, then, that in the Overprotective Parent vs. Helpless Child relationship, both people need to change to effect a positive outcome for their relationship. Helpless Mates need to affirm their identities as separate from their loved ones. Overprotective Mates need to give up the role of parents and let their partners grow up as individuals in their own right. Once this is achieved, the 80/20 balance becomes closer to 50/50. The overt and covert resentment, on both sides, dissipates and is replaced by more positive, caring feelings.

nagging parent versus irresponsible child

As we saw in the last chapter, this relationship is one in which one partner (Irresponsible Child) controls the relationship by acting in inappropriate and irresponsible ways personally, professionally and/or socially. The counterpart mate, the Nagging Mate, often starts out submissive and passive, in the hope that the irresponsible partner will change, but, discouraged and fed up, often begins to alternate this behavior with nagging and bitching. Over time, each one's behavior becomes more pronounced. The result is the couple grows further apart, with many angry, hurt feelings on both sides.

Bob and Sharon have been married for twenty years and have one son who is sixteen years old. Bob is a successful real estate developer. Sharon was an elementary school teacher in the early years of their marriage, but for the last seven or eight years has not worked and has stayed home. Now that their son is older, Sharon has had little to do at home. For the last several years, Bob has had an affair with a secretary at his office. In the four months prior to counseling, Sharon found out about the affair and nagged Bob repeatedly about his "responsibilities" to her and their family, but to no avail. He has continued the affair. During the course of this affair, Bob has spent a great deal of money on this other woman. In fact, even though he has made a considerable amount of money each year, Bob spends almost all of it, often frivolously. In the past he has gone into a department or clothing store and spent $1,000 during his lunch hour. As a result, he and Sharon, now in their late forties, own only their home and have no other assets.

Bob grew up in a home where his mother was permissive and overindulgent. His wife followed the same pattern. Though Sharon nags Bob a great deal, she in fact passively and submissively accepts his irresponsible behavior; in short, she puts no real, concrete limits on Bob's behavior.

When couple counseling was initiated with Bob and Sharon, Bob was still having the affair, spending a large amount of money, and having temper tantrums when he didn't get his way. Sharon was fairly unhappy in her own life. She was not working, her sixteen-year-old son was quite independent, and she had little to do all day but feel depressed and worry about Bob's infidelity.

The main treatment strategy was to get Sharon to change her behavior. Though Sharon nagged Bob, she really didn't follow through or set limits on Bob's behavior. Moreover, her nagging caused her to feel guilty and she would then become quite passive, letting Bob do as he pleased for a period of time. It took several months of counseling before Sharon had the confidence to be assertive with Bob and to apply consequences, not words, to Bob's irresponsible behavior.

In the past, Sharon had implored Bob to stop his affair with his secretary on the grounds that it was immoral and personally upsetting to her, all to no avail. Using consequences, not words, one day Sharon packed Bob's bags and told him to go to a motel for three days and make up his mind whether he wanted to stay married or get divorced. He was not to return home unless he would end his affair. Two days later, Bob came home and said he would terminate his involvement with his secretary — and he did. The next week he found his secretary another job and he didn't see her after that.

With respect to their financial problems, which resulted from Bob's foolish spending, it was agreed that Sharon would take over the finances and plan their investments. She put Bob on a weekly allowance, which he stuck by, and with the extra money she began to invest wisely.

In the past, when Bob didn't want to go to work, he told his wife to go out and tell his ride he was ill. He then took the day off and stayed home. Sharon had always obediently done as Bob told her. If she protested at all, he had a temper tantrum, yelled and screamed, and threw his briefcase on the floor. Sharon nagged, but always gave in. As Sharon learned to be assertive, she simply put her foot down and told Bob to go to work or tell his ride himself that he was not going. The result was that Bob went to work. Over time Sharon's assertiveness and her setting limits with consequences on Bob's behavior got him to act more responsibly.

Therapy also helped Sharon to see that she was overly involved in Bob's life and not meeting her own needs. Sharon decided to go back to work. She got a job teaching, which helped her build her self-confidence and made her feel less dependent on Bob. This increased self-confidence, in turn, allowed her to be more confident in being assertive and setting limits on Bob. Sharon had always feared that Bob would divorce her if she stood up to him, since in the past he had often threatened to do so if he didn't get his way. Now she discovered that her assertive behavior did not in fact alienate Bob, and, with the discovery, she became more comfortable with being assertive. It seemed Bob was even more attracted to her as a result of her assertiveness and limit-setting.

Working with a couple where one partner is irresponsible and gets away with it, as Bob had done, is almost impossible without change on the part of the more responsible mate. Sharon's changing her nagging behavior to assertiveness, and following through with behavioral consequences, was the key to changing their marriage. They also went from an 80/20 split to more nearly a 50/50 marriage.

Helping Bob to see the difference between responsible and irresponsible behavior as well as the value of postponing his immediate needs for a more substantial reinforcement later on, also helped him become more responsible. This insight probably would not have been very beneficial, however, had he not had his wife to set realistic but appropriate limits on his behavior.

If couples in the Nagging vs. Irresponsible Partner pattern are to be helped, the Nagging Mates must come to realize they can, in fact, live without their partners. They need to know they can survive on their own. This realization effectively eliminates their irresponsible partners often-voiced threat to leave if they don't get their way. After acquiring self-confidence, the Nagging Mate can learn to be assertive and to set consequences on the Irresponsible

Mate's behavior. This changes an 80/20 relationship to one more nearly 50/50. Also, the Irresponsible Partner can learn the difference between responsible and irresponsible behavior and work towards meeting goals via responsible behavior. Marital therapy was successful in Bob's and Sharon's case; they like themselves and each other better as a result of these changes. My experience is that if the Nagging Passive Mate can change, then there is a good chance to restructure the relationship for a positive outcome. If Sharon had been unable to change, if she had not come to believe that she could live without her husband, become more assertive, and set limits on Bob's behavior and stick to them, however, the chances that Bob would have changed his irresponsible behavior on his own would have been highly unlikely.

summary

Overall, there are three general strategies for improving a relationship with someone you love.

The first way to improve you love relationship is to *deal successfully with five critical issues* all couples face in their relationship with one another: 1) interpersonal communication skills (giving and assertion); 2) sexual compatibility; 3) successful resolution of conflict; 4) development of emotional intimacy; 5) learning to have fun together.

The second way to improve a love relationship is to *deal specifically with any aspect of your relationship that you consider self-defeating in nature*. You do this by evaluating what is wrong with your relationship. Is there a lopsided balance of power (80/20)? Are you engaging in rigid role-playing? Do you have a self-defeating interactive pattern (e.g., Angry vs. Appeasing Partner)? Once you evaluate your relationship, then you can take concrete steps to correct the problem.

The final way is to *work on yourself* a bit, to make yourself healthier and more fulfilled as a person. You may need to change and grow as a person in your own right. For example, if you lack self-confidence, there are specific things you can do to enhance your feelings about yourself. If you are not meeting your needs, you can take active steps to correct this situation. Specifically, the next section deals with ways you can increase your own self-esteem and meet your own needs in a more efficient manner.

PART THREE

Enhancing the Love Relationship via Self-Love

9

four basic psychological needs

introduction

Up to this point we have stressed skills couples can engage in jointly with each other to enhance the quality of their love relationship. In this final section, we will explore skills each of you can initiate on your own to feel better about yourself as a person. As a result you should be able to love yourself more.

It cannot be overemphasized that true love of others is predicated on the notion that you first love yourself. Before you can be successful in an adult male/female relationship, you need to feel good about yourself.

Chances are, the better you feel about yourself, the easier it will be to love someone else and also to accept the love offered you. Also, the more healthy you are in a psychological sense, the healthier a mate you will pick. The opposite is also true. If you feel unhappy and miserable in your life, you are more likely to pick someone who is also unhappy and dissatisfied. Most often, opposites do not attract in this regard. It is more likely for couples to be of equal psychological well-being. It stands to reason, then, that the healthier and happier you are, the healthier a mate you will select and the healthier a relationship you can develop.

Learning to love yourself is no easy task, and as an adult it takes some hard, diligent work on your part. Most of us have heard the proverbial, "you can't love someone else until you learn to love yourself." But few people know how to go about learning to love themselves more.

In these last two chapters, you will learn what it takes to become more compassionate toward yourself and what steps you can actually take to feel more self-accepting and loving.

In this chapter you will learn about four basic psychological needs all human beings possess. If these needs can be met on some consistent basis, you will have gone a long way to feeling happier, less stressed, and more self-accepting and content.

human needs

All human beings have needs that must be met for survival as a species. Human needs can be broken down into three broad areas: Biological-Survival Needs, Psychological Needs, and Spiritual Needs.

Biological-Survival Needs include the requirements for food, clothing, shelter, and a sense of security. These basic needs have to be met or human beings simply cannot go on living. Moreover, Biological-Survival Needs have to be fulfilled to some degree before any other needs can be met.

The other needs are not absolutely necessary for physical survival but define the quality of social survival as human beings. Psychological Needs have to do with being close to and relating successfully to other people, being your own person, having your own identity, feeling a sense of achievement by accomplishment and, finally, relaxing and enjoying leisure activities. The final category of needs, Spiritual Needs, includes spiritual life and an individual's personal relationship with God.

Although no one would deny that a part of the male-female love relationship can be related to Biological-Survival Needs, and indeed Spiritual Needs as well, this section will be devoted to the male-female relationship as it relates to Psychological Needs. I do not mean to underplay the significance of the other needs, especially the spiritual needs. Rather, this orientation simply reflects my own training as a psychologist and marital therapist.

psychological needs

As we have seen, each person has four psychological needs that must be met throughout life. These four needs are:

1. The need for close, loving relationships.
2. The need for autonomy and independence as a person.
3. The need to achieve and be successful.
4. The need for play and fun.

Each of these four basic needs is present at birth or shortly thereafter and remains throughout the life cycle. Also, each of these four needs manifests itself somewhat differently at each developmental stage of growth. For example, the Relationship Need for a newborn infant is to receive maternal love (holding, cuddling, and protection). However, the same Relationship Need for an adolescent boy may be to have a parent listen with concern and support to his frustration at not getting a starting position on the high school basketball team. For an adult, the Relationship Need often is expressed in dating, engagement, and marriage. So the same Relationship Need is present on all three occasions but is expressed differently at different ages. As we look at these four needs, we will discuss only how they appear for adults.*

the relationship need

The Relationship Need is the need for close, intimate relations with other human beings. It is the need for love, attention, support, acceptance, and belonging.

All people want to be close to other people. Adults seek out relationships in which they can fulfill their romantic sexual needs. They want to fall in love and be in love. In addition to being in love, the Relationship Need includes the desire to be understood, listened to, and accepted by others. It also includes people's desire to feel that the relationships they are involved in are genuine, and that other people are honest and open with them.

The Relationship Need can be better understood if broken down into two broad areas: friendship and intimacy.

Friendship includes the need to feel a sense of belonging with other human beings. It is the desire to be accepted, supported, and approved of by others. It reflects the desire to socialize with others on an enjoyable, comfortable basis. In short, friendship reflects the need to be with people and do things with people.

Intimacy reflects the desire to relate to other human beings at a deeper, more emotional level. Here people want to feel they are really heard and understood, that they can share their real selves and that they will be accepted for who they are. They also want to be able to give of themselves and know that they will be accepted and that their giving will enrich the lives of others. Moreover, they want to spend time and have fun with those they love. So the Relationship Need involves the need to relate to, give to and receive from others.

* For a more detailed explanation of the four basic Psychological Needs in a developmental context, and as they relate to the parent-child relationship, see *IMPACT Parent Training: Becoming a Successful Parent*, by E.M. Lillibridge and Andrew G. Mathirs, published by Marriage Encounter, Inc., 1982.

autonomy-independence need

The Relationship Need primarily involves love, approval, and acceptance from "significant others." The Relationship Need is interpersonal in that it involves another person. It is usually positive and brings people closer together. The Autonomy-Independence Need, however, does not really involve other people in the same way as the Relationship Need does. The Autonomy-Independence Need is the need to be your own person, separate and distinct from others. This need often involves asserting yourself against other people and expressing your own wants and desires.

This need really begins at about the time a young child is two years old. Here, for the first time, children see themselves as different from other people and want to do things on their own, separate from their parents. In many parent books, this phase is called "the terrible twos." Children begin to feel their power as individuals, and saying "no" or resisting their parents is a way of asserting their own personalities.

Again, like the Relationship Need, the need to be autonomous and independent is a need everyone has throughout life. This need operates on two levels. First, on a day-to-day basis, anytime you state a preference for this over that, whether it's a certain meal, the choice of a movie, or how you want to spend some leisure time, you are asserting your preference as a person as to what is right for you. So, day to day, you regularly assert your need to be your own person, based on your values, your choices, and your preferences.

Second, at certain developmental stages, the need for individual identity often becomes a prominent, if not the most important, fact in life. A two year old's "resistance" to parental authority is impulsive, immature, and often inappropriate by adult standards, but it is healthy for the young child to develop this separateness and sense of individual identity. Another very important developmental stage for the Autonomy-Independence Need occurs in adolescence, when the child again becomes assertive, often resistant, in preparation for breaking away from the family and beginning a more separate life. Adolescents also begin to seek their own identities, defining for themselves their values, their interests, and their desires. Adolescents striving for independence are often troubled by mixed feelings. They want to be totally on their own and treated like adults, but at the same time they desire the security of the family. Adolescence can be a difficult time for both the child and the parent.

Another developmental stage where the Autonomy-Independence Need is more pronounced is in young adulthood, when a career choice must be made, mate selection considered, and the initiation of families determined.

Again, the emphasis in on "What do *I* want to do with my life?" (via a career, marriage, family).

The midlife transition phase involves reexamining the choices of career, mate, and lifestyle made as young adults. Like adolescence, this is often a time of inner turmoil which often involves a questioning of values and identities. Out of the decisions made can come new growth and life changes.

Finally, retirement from job or career poses problems and potential benefits. Again, the question is "What will *I* do with my life now?" This involves how leisure time is spent, how to face death, and how to relate to others in the new role of winding down life.

Thus, at certain developmental stages (i.e., adolescence, young adulthood, middle age) Autonomy-Independence Needs are more pronounced. In addition, on a daily basis Autonomy-Independence Needs involve asserting individual rights and preferences. But the main issue at stake in both instances is personal identity. Your sense of identity comes from knowing who you are and being able to be yourself.

Let us take a moment to examine the relationship between the need for others (Relationship Need) and the need to be yourself (Autonomy-Independence Need) before going on.

Every human being has to juggle and find a balance between these two needs to be happy. You cannot sacrifice one for the other without paying a price in terms of your self-esteem and your ability to love yourself. If, for example, your need for approval, love, and support of others (the Relationship Need) becomes absolutely critical (that is, life cannot go on without it), then you begin to do anything and everything to please others, thinking it will insure that others will like and accept you. You will do most anything to get the approval of others, obviously neglecting your own needs (Autonomy-Independence). You do not assert yourself with others, fearing rejection.

What usually happens, however, is that this plan backfires. The simple fact is that people will lose respect for you if you act as if you don't respect yourself. They will not give you the approval you seek, but rather will take you for granted and, in fact, often take advantage of you.

Moreover, if you don't assert yourself and instead spend all your time trying to please others, you lose touch with yourself. You begin to lose your sense of personal identity. If you don't have a clear sense of your own identity, others can't really like you because they sense that you don't really like yourself. You can also find yourself becoming frustrated because you are not doing those things you like and enjoy.

To go in the opposite direction, however, and to meet Autonomy-Independence Needs exclusively while ignoring Relationship Needs, also creates problems. If you decide it is critically important to be yourself at all costs, you may choose to tell people what you want and do what you want, no matter how it affects them. The result will be that you may have a clear sense of who you are as a person but you may also be very lonely. If you act just in your own self-interest, you are usually going to ignore the needs of others. They will then perceive you as selfish and be reluctant to form close relationships with you. The consequence will be that you receive no support, understanding, or love from others because they have no desire to be taken advantage of by you.

Clearly, everyone needs to learn how to meet *both* sets of needs — the need for personal identity and the need to be close to and relate to other people on an intimate level. Further, to enjoy a healthy relationship, both parties need a comfortable balance between both sets of needs. Often in the self-defeating relationship, this balance is lopsided. For example, with the Angry vs. Appeasing Mate, the Appeasing Partner is overly invested in the Relationship Need and low on Autonomy-Independence Needs. The Angry Mate is the opposite.

If both needs are met, however, each need is strengthened by the other. If you love and accept others, you will feel good about yourself. And if you are happy and secure with yourself, you will naturally move toward other people in a supportive, caring manner.

achievement need

The third basic need, Achievement, is somewhat closely aligned with the need for Autonomy-Independence. The Achievement Need is the desire to do the best you can at something and to feel a sense of accomplishment, while at the same time gaining recognition from others for what you have done. This need usually starts by ages eight to twelve. Around this time, children begin to devote their time and attention to something like scholastic achievement, sports, or special projects. They want to be good at something and gain recognition for their achievement.

The Achievement Need grows stronger in adolescence and in early adulthood, and is usually the basis for wanting to develop a career or occupation. At first, the desire for achievement is fostered by the desire for social recognition and approval (Relationship Need) and, in addition, by the desire for independence as a separate person (Autonomy Need). As time goes by, this desire to achieve is internalized, and accomplishment and proficiency become rewarding in and of themselves. The child might desire to be a good swimmer, an accomplished saxophonist, or a straight A student. An adult might desire to be a lawyer, a writer, or a teacher. Achieving and accomplishing something — whatever it might be — gives you a good feeling about yourself and helps build a positive self-image.

Again, this too is a lifelong need, becoming most pronounced in adulthood. Once there is a real sense of accomplishment in career goals, the desire to achieve often gets funneled into avocational pursuits. This is especially true in retirement.

play-fun need

A fourth need demonstrated by the human organism begins in childhood and remains constant throughout the life cycle. This is the need for Fun and Play. Play is something that you can engage in alone or with someone else. Who has not watched with delight a young child absorbed in fantasy and imaginary play, play-acting the roles of several people talking to each other? Or seen adolescent girls and boys talking, laughing, teasing as they flirt and joke with each other? Adults engage in games and sports, socialize with friends, go to concerts, take walks on the beach. Play allows people the opportunity to relax, and provides a change of pace so that they may more fully enjoy themselves and experience pleasure in their lives. In short, the Play-Fun Need is the desire for leisure time. It is necessary if people are to be happy and well-adjusted.

As we said earlier, there is an interplay between the Autonomy-Independence Need and the Relationship Need. There is also an interplay between the Achievement Need and the Play-Fun Need. It is important here also that people achieve a balance between these two needs. Focusing on just the Achievement Need (working night and day to have a successful career) would inevitably mean sacrificing Play-Fun Needs, which would create stress. Many people who are workaholics do just this: they overstress the Achievement Needs to the exclusion of their other three basic needs, especially neglecting the time needed for leisure and relaxation in their lives.

Those who try just the opposite and attempt to meet only Play-Fun Needs and neglect Achievement Needs, however, also run into problems. Who has not heard someone (perhaps even yourself?) make the casual remark: "I would be completely happy never to work again. I'd love just to sit at the beach all day and do nothing." Such a comment is usually tossed off after a hard day's work. When people actually try to devote their entire lives to nothing but relaxation and play, however, thereby giving up their Achievement Needs, they generally develop a low-grade depression. People often experience this depression when they first retire because they no longer feel challenged by anything. They have nothing to commit themselves to, to work hard at, and from which to gain a sense of accomplishment and recognition. So, again, it is critical to strike a balance between Achievement Needs, for the recognition and the feeling of accomplishment it provides, and Play-Fun Needs, for relaxation and enjoyment.

meeting all four needs

Although it is important to achieve a balance between all needs, at certain times an individual will focus on one need more than the others. For example, a student just starting medical school, or an executive just being promoted to a new and challenging job, or a housewife going back to work after the children are raised, will each spend a great deal of time on Achievement Needs and will probably neglect the other needs for awhile. Or a couple just dating and falling in love for the first time will be concerned with Relationship Needs and forget about everything else. Anyone who has worked long and hard at a job all year will certainly want to relax and do no work while on vacation, letting Fun-Play Needs dominate thought and time. This overemphasis on one need at certain times and under certain circumstances is normal and understandable.

It is also important to recognize that engaging in one activity can facilitate meeting all four needs. For example, a few years ago I took up sailing when I was seeking something new and different in my life. I had never sailed before and my motive for sailing at first related to my Autonomy-Independence Needs. I wanted to sail; it was a new and exciting challenge to me. I felt I was asserting myself in a new area of my life. My focus was on myself and the fact I was doing something new. After I learned to sail and overcame initial fear and apprehension concerning the techniques of sailing, sailing became more focused on my Fun-Play Needs. I went to the beach to sail, relax, and be in the sun. After a while I joined a sailing club and began to enter regattas. My Achievement Needs took over. I now wanted not just to sail but to sail well and to compete with others. Finally, the sailing club provided me with a new social group in which new friendships developed, thus meeting some of my Relationship Needs. So one activity, in this case sailing, was able to meet my four basic psychological needs.

The first step in learning to feel better about yourself is the recognition that everyone has four basic psychological needs, and the goal is to meet *all four* needs, not just one or two.

110

a self-assessment
exercise of psychological needs

In the following section, there are some specific questions about each of the four basic psychological needs. The questions are not designed to be comprehensive in nature but, rather, to get you to think about these needs in more personal terms. The point of this exercise is to help you assess the degree to which you might or might not be meeting your needs.

Following each set of questions is a brief paragraph or two describing the common difficulties most people have in meeting that specific need. If you are having difficulty meeting any one of these needs, this section might give you some clues as to the reason.

Relationship Need (Love, approval, acceptance, stroking, friendship, companionship)

1. Can you socialize and meet people easily? __ yes __ no
2. Do you feel the need always to please others or do what they want to do? __ yes __ no
3. Do you have a close intimate relationship now? __ yes __ no
4. If you answered yes to (3), is this relationship working smoothly at present? __ yes __ no
5. Do you have friends who you feel accept you as your are and not for what you could become? __ yes __ no

The goal here is to have the capacity to socialize with people and to be intimate with others.

Problems usually develop when you are uncomfortable meeting and socializing with people. The underlying fear is that you will be rejected by others. The fear of rejection often leads to two types of behavior: shyness, avoiding others so as to escape painful rejection; or people-pleasing behavior, doing anything and everything for others, hoping desperately you can please them and they will not reject you.

Your goal should be to take the appropriate and necessary risks so that you can get close to people and meet your Relationship Needs.

Autonomy-Independence Needs (Being your own person, being able to be assertive with others)

1. Can you be assertive and disagree with people you are close to? __ yes __ no
2. Can you be assertive with people you are not close to (casual friends, salesmen, car mechanics, etc.)? __ yes __ no
3. If you are afraid of something that you want to do, do you do it any-

way or avoid it?   __ do it __ avoid it
4. Do you make your own decisions or rely on others to help you make
   decisions?   __ make own decisions __ others make decision
5. Are your currently doing what you want to do with your life?
                                                                   __ yes __ no

Your Autonomy-Independence Needs have to do with making your own decisions and standing up for your rights by being assertive with others. They also have to do with developing a sense of self-confidence by facing and doing things we fear doing but want to do (e.g., overcoming a fear of public speaking or flying). The more you do these things, the more self-reliant and self-accepting you become.

Achievement Needs (Striving to accomplish things to the best of your ability)

1. Do you have a job that is stimulating and rewarding?
                                                                   __ yes __ no
2. Do you put off doing things on your job?   __ yes __ no
3. Do you work so much that you don't enjoy your job?
                                                                   __ yes __ no
4. List several things your are currently working on that are challenging
   and exciting (projects, job, new skills).

   A. _____
   B. _____
   C. _____
   D. _____

There are two clues to possible difficulties in the Achievement area. First, if you find that you have a perfectionist attitude toward yourself and your work, that you are demanding too much from yourself, then you are likely to become a workaholic. Second, if you are overly fearful of failure and decide to avoid difficult tasks or projects, then you will procrastinate when it comes to getting jobs done. So it's important to work towards accepting challenges and achieving something you value, and to try to avoid getting bogged down by fears of failure or demanding too much from yourself.

Play-Fun Needs (Rest, Relaxation, Leisure Time)

1. Do you have hobbies and activities that are relaxing and
   enjoyable?   __ yes __ no
2. List five to ten things you do for fun.

   A. _____
   B. _____
   C. _____
   D. _____

E. _____

F. _____

G. _____

H. _____

I. _____

J. _____

3. Now, beside each activity you listed, put the last time you engaged in this activity.

Often, several things can interfere with your taking and enjoying leisure time. For example, it will be impossible to meet your Fun-Play Needs if you overstress your Achievement Needs and don't find time to relax. Another thing that can interfere with your enjoying leisure time is making all the activities you enjoy highly competitive. Competition is at times fun as well as appropriate, but when all your activities are competitive in nature — when it's only fun to play tennis or racquetball if you win, for instance — you are not really meeting your Fun-Play Needs. You are substituting the Fun-Play Need with an overemphasis on competition. So, it is important to find activities that help you relax and enjoy yourself, and to do them on a regular basis with the focus on *pleasure* rather than on winning at all costs.

This exercise on your basic psychological needs was meant to help stimulate your thinking about how well you might be meeting or not meeting these needs. You can go a long way toward feeling better about yourself by working hard to meet all four of these needs.

summary

This chapter has emphasized the importance of the four basic Psychological Needs in life. If you are willing to work at it a bit, you can learn to meet these needs. Learning to meet *all* these needs: getting close to people, being yourself as a person, working to the best of your ability at something, and learning to relax and play, will make you feel better and more positive about yourself as a person.

My colleague, Dr. Andrew Mathirs, and I have developed a psychological inventory that attempts to measure how effectively people are meeting these four basic psychological needs.* We have found that if these needs are met in a consistent fashion, self-esteem and self-acceptance increase. When individuals are blocked off from meeting even one need, it adversely affects their sense of self-worth. When people can be helped by therapy or other means to meet needs they have not been meeting, their self-esteem increases.

---

* For information regarding this personal assessment inventory (PAI) and the Computer Print-Out Interpretation, write the author at University Professional Center / 3500 E. Fletcher Avenue / Suite 509 / Tampa, Florida 33612.

Fulfilling these psychological needs thus will carry you a long way toward learning to love and accept yourself. Self-love and self-acceptance in turn help you build a healthy love relationship.

10
building positive self-esteem

In Chapter Nine, one of the four basic Psychological Needs we examined was the Autonomy-Independence Need, reflecting not only the desire to be separate and distinct from others but also the desire to pursue a course of action based on personal values and goals. This achievement of the Autonomy-Independence Need greatly helps people develop thier individual identities and stimulates their sense of self-esteem.

In this chapter we will explore how self-esteem may be enhanced. Self-esteem is made up of two major components: one, the attitudes that you hold about yourself and, two, the behavior you engage in. Attitudes and behavior can either enhance or detract from feelings of self-esteem.

positive attitudes

Let's first examine some of the attitudes that are necessary to gain not only positive self-esteem but greater self-acceptance as well.

Perfectionism. One of the biggest hindrances to building positive self-esteem is the expectation of perfection, the setting of incredibly high standards for personal performance that are basically unrealistic and unattainable. Unfortunately, too many people tend to think in such perfectionistic terms as "I will not be pleased with my performance until it's perfect" or "practice makes perfect" or "if you can't do it right, don't do it at all." If you believe such statements, you will find it impossible to achieve anything, because human beings are fallible and can never really be perfect at anything.

If you believe in perfectionism, you are saying that you can't love yourself until you have done something flawlessly. Self-acceptance is therefore withheld until something has been done or accomplished in just the desired way. But human beings, by nature, are prone to make mistakes at times, and will never achieve perfection. If you can't accept this reality, you will be in great inner turmoil much of the time. This inner turmoil is usually reflected in self-critical and self-castigating remarks meant to "shape us up," but which on the contrary lead to a "poorer" performance and loss of self-esteem. Note the following example.

Margie was twenty-five, married, and had no children when she came to me for counseling. At the time she entered treatment, she was a whirlwind of activity. She was a full-time student at the university, worked twenty hours a week at a part-time job, was conducting research on a Master's Thesis, and was an active member of several school organizations (being the president of one of them). Not only that, but she also cleaned the house and cooked all the meals for herself and her husband. To the casual observer, Margie looked happy and busy; inside, however, she was tormented because nothing she did was good enough for her. She was constantly berating her performance in everything she undertook: her grades weren't good enough (she was an A-B student); her house wasn't clean enough (her husband reported the house was immaculate); she did a poor job as president of her organization (she had received high praise from faculty and fellow students for her hard work); and on and on the self-criticism went. In short, Margie was a perfectionist; she was extremely self-critical and prone to depression if she wasn't continuously working and succeeding at something. She couldn't relax and meet her Fun-Play Needs because that was "wasting time." She felt she should be doing something more important and worthwhile.

Over the course of many months, Margie had to learn to let go of her perfectionism and accept for herself more realistic and appropriate standards and goals. It was only then that she could really begin to like and eventually love and accept herself. As this case shows, perfectionism can be a major block to learning to love yourself.

The first positive attitude you should strive for, then, is to have realistic perceptions about yourself and to set realistic, not perfectionistic, standards for your performance.

Fear of Failure. Perfectionism often leads to workaholic behavior, as was the case with Margie, because you think that with just a little more work you will get it just right. Fear of failure is the other side of the coin of perfectionism. Here the fear of failing or making a mistake leads to procrastination and avoiding the work at hand. Again, avoidance behavior leads to a loss of self-esteem. What you need to realize is that failing at something is normal. Everybody does it. Most people make about twenty mistake a day, large and small. If you can't accept the fact that you will make mistakes, you will end up hating yourself and will get little, if anything, accomplished in your life.

Fear of failure can literally paralyze many people. Fearful of doing something because they either have to be perfect or can't tolerate making a mistake, they end up completely stymied. Both perfectionism and fear of failure often indirectly interfere with Achievement Needs.

Take the case of Nancy. She was married and had one small child who had recently reached school age. Nancy was faced with a big void in her life when her only child started school and, at the same time, she gave up a part-time volunteer job she had held for several years.

Nancy was offered several well-paying jobs as a result of her excellent work in the volunteer organization. She turned them all down, however, saying in therapy that she was terrified of taking a "real job" for pay. She equated working for money with a new set of standards for herself, namely that she couldn't make mistakes. Nancy was obsessed about never making an error. She was constantly trying to anticipate and correct problems before they even occurred.

Her fear of failing directly affected her self-esteem. She wanted to work because she had gained great satisfaction from her volunteer efforts. But her fear of failure had paralyzed her, and she had become caustic and self-critical for not going out and getting a paying job. Her inability to take a job — even a job she thought she'd enjoy — led to guilt and depression. Nancy needed to learn not to equate making mistakes or failing at something with her personal self-worth. She needed to learn that everyone makes mistakes and that making mistakes is part of being human. Nancy needed to learn to *accept* her mistakes, faults, and foibles, and to realize that she could also learn from them and thus reduce the chances of making the same errors in the future. Your goal when dealing with your all-too-human errors is to learn from them rather than criticizing or belittling yourself, since that will only lead to guilt and depression.

If not dealt with appropriately, both perfectionism and fear of failure can be lethal blows to self-esteem and learning to love yourself.

Learning From Failure. Learning from failure ties in with both perfectionism and the fear of failure. Both successful and unsuccessful people make mistakes. One of the big differences between successful and unsuccessful people, however, is that successful people accept their mistakes as part of being human. They learn what they can from their mistakes, then forget them and go on with life. They don't dwell on their "goofs" and failures. Unsuccessful people do the opposite. They overfocus on their mistakes and ignore their accomplishments.

If you fail at something, you can react in one of two ways. You can be self-critical and blame yourself, saying "I'll never try this again" or "What a dumbbell I am." This approach usually leads to more self-criticism, depression, and guilt, and often to either avoidance or attempts at overachievement as a compensation. Or you can react to your failure by adopting a problem-solving model. When you make a mistake, you accept it and then ask yourself what went wrong? Can it be corrected? If it can't be changed or undone, accept it and go on. If it can be corrected, discover the best way of doing so and then implement a strategy for appropriate change immediately. The key is to avoid self-blame and focus instead on correcting the problem.

Both Nancy and Margie had to learn to be less self-critical; they had to learn to focus less on themselves and more on the problem at hand. Once they had done everything to correct a problem or error, they learned to drop it and go on with their lives. The results were less guilt, depression, and self-anger, and eventually more self-acceptance and self-love.

Praising Yourself. Learning to praise yourself means developing a positive attitude toward yourself. Very often people are quick to criticize themselves for the mistakes they make while, at the same time, ignoring the things they do well. They would do better at times to reverse this process and to ignore some of their mistakes while positively reinforcing their accomplishments. Most people find it easy to praise the accomplishments of others, but have great difficulty giving themselves an honest pat on the back.

Everyone needs to give him or herself positive strokes and tangible rewards for the good work he or she does. A positive stroke is simply a self-statement that reflects a job well done. For example, after you have written a difficult report or finished a particularly hard job, you simply say to yourself: "That was a hard job and I did it very well. I am proud of the way I handled it." At first, saying such things can seem conceited or maybe artificial. But remember, praising your own personal legitimate accomplishments is just as important as praising the successes of others. Such self-praise helps people to learn how to feel better about themselves.

You can also reinforce yourself by giving yourself tangible rewards. For instance, you may want to give yourself a special treat (i.e., a favorite meal at a good restaurant, a long hot shower, a night on the town, or even a weekend vacation). These rewards reinforce you in the work you do and are concrete manifestations that you like yourself and deserve such rewards for doing well. If you don't like yourself, you will rarely if ever reward yourself for anything you might accomplish.

Both Nancy and Margie had to learn to praise and tangibly reward themselves. Each had a tendency to discount any of their successes by finding some minor fault or imperfection in anything they accomplished. At first, learning to praise and positively reinforce themselves made them feel awkward and undeserving. With time, patience, and quite a bit of practice, however, each was better able to enjoy and accept her legitimate successes.

Therefore, if you can be realistic and not perfectionistic in your appraisal of yourself, not be terrified of failure but be willing to learn from your mistakes, and learn to praise yourself, you will have a positive attitude that will enhance your self-esteem and self-acceptance.

positive behaviors

Obviously, the attitudes individuals hold about themselves greatly influence their perceptions of themselves. Attitudes that are congruent with reality lead to a realistic self-appraisal and subsequently to positive self-esteem. When the attitudes individuals hold about themselves are not in line with reality, as with the case of perfectionists, they will be impossible to live up to, and self-esteem invariably plummets. Behavior, like attitudes, can either enhance or hinder self-esteem.

Being Alone. One of the first things that anyone can do behaviorally to enhance the capacity for self-acceptance and self-esteem is to spend time alone. It is important to be alone both physically and emotionally. Being physically alone means spending time by yourself, separate from other people. It could be taking a weekend alone at the beach, bike-riding by yourself, jogging for an hour alone. The idea is to be able to be by yourself, away from others. This time gives you the opportunity to reflect on your life, to get to know yourself better, and to become more self-reliant.

Being alone emotionally refers to being more reliant upon yourself rather than upon others. If you can't be alone, your self-perceptions become heavily influenced by what others think of you, and as a result you tend to form overly-dependent relationships. In a dependent relationship, instead of *wanting* to be with someone you *need* to be with them. This need quickly creates an 80/20 relationship.

I have worked in therapy with many couples experiencing marital problems who report that never in their lives have they been on their own. One woman reported she always had a boyfriend, from junior high school on through high school and college. She didn't end one relationship until she had already formed another. When I saw her, she was having difficulty in her second marriage. She had met her present husband while still married to her first husband. When she separated from her second husband at age thirty-three, for the first time in her life she was totally alone emotionally. She was terrified because she felt she had to have someone. This belief had always led her into dependent relationships with men, in which she needed men but, at the same time, also resented them. She needed to learn to be comfortably alone, by herself, as a prerequisite to forming a successful love relationship.

Being alone, both emotionally (i.e., not dependent on the constant approval of others) and physically (i.e., spending time away from other people), is a first big step to becoming more self-reliant. As people become more self-reliant, they become more self-accepting and self-loving. The concept of being alone does not mean, however, that everyone should become a hermit and avoid other people or that the opinions and approval of others should be given no importance. Rather, it means that you should be comfortable with yourself as a person and that you are able to spend time alone. A useful exercise in this regard is to take some time off and get away by yourself, whether it's just for a few hours or for a weekend. It's one of the best ways to get to know yourself better.

Self-Respect. Being alone allows you to become less dependent on others and more aware of yourself and what you value as a person. As you identify and become aware of your values and what's important to you, then living up to those values becomes a significant issue. Your ability to do so will be a significant factor in your self-respect.

The concept of self-respect involves two variables: values and behavior. For you to feel a healthy sense of self-respect, your values and your behavior must coincide. For example, if you value honesty and openness in interpersonal relations and yet find yourself being deceitful and manipulative, then you will lose respect for yourself because you are not living up to your values. If, on the other hand, you value honesty in your intimate relations and you are in fact genuine and real in interpersonal interactions, then you will feel a sense of positive self-respect. Positive self-respect comes, then, from the degree to which your values and your behavior coincide.

Don was experiencing a loss of self-respect when he came for psychotherapy. He described himself as always having been known as a "straight shooter" at his job. He always gave his honest opinions, never minced words, and could be counted on to cut through the baloney and call a situation as he saw it. Don liked this image of himself and his behavior was congruent with his image. Two years before Don was to retire, he got a new boss whose style and temperament were the opposite of his own. Don found that if he was honest and forthright about problem areas, he was harshly criticized by his boss. His new supervisor was not comfortable with Don's straightforward approach.

As the relationship became more strained between the two, Don felt — for the first time in his career — that he could be fired and his retirement benefits could be jeopardized. With this realization, Don began to keep his ideas to himself. In his own mind, he became something of a "yes man" with his superior. Over a six-month period, his relationship with his boss improved, but Don felt he was not being himself. He was losing his self-respect because his behavior and his values no longer matched. During this period Don began drinking more and feeling quite depressed. As he became aware of the problem, Don finally decided to change jobs within the plant and to work for a former supervisor with whom he felt he could be himself. This switch allowed Don to gain back the self-respect he had been losing.

A valuable exercise is to assess your major values and the degree to which you are meeting them. It may help you to determine you values to refer back to the last chapter on the four basic Psychological Needs (Relationship, Autonomy-Independence, Achievement and Play). Most values lie in these areas. For example, if you value honesty in relationships, you are referring to your Autonomy-Independence Needs and your Relationship Needs. If you believe taking care of yourself via leisure time is an important value in terms of reducing stress in your life, you are referring to your Play-Fun Needs. Assessing your major values — what's really important to you — and then comparing the results to your behavior — what you actually do — will tell you a great deal about your own self-respect.

After you assess what you value and what you are doing in the area you value, you might write down what concrete steps you can take to bring your values and your behavior in line with one another. Taking these concrete steps is what will enhance your self-respect. A word of caution: if you have a perfectionistic attitude or believe you can't make mistakes, you will be setting yourself up for a "Catch-22" in which you will never be able to live up to your values, no matter what you do. So, if you decide to change some of your behavior, set realistic goals for yourself and allow for errors along the way.

Self-Confidence. Self-confidence refers to that inner strength which results from the belief that you can handle new and difficult situations. Specifically, you tend to develop self-confidence when you face the things you fear doing (but often want to do), and do something constructive about them. For example, several years ago I was very fearful of flying in airplanes and tended to avoid it at all costs. As a result of this avoidance, I seldom saw my parents and my sisters who live across the country, rejected numerous consulting jobs, and turned down several nice vacations. Of course, my fear of flying increased the more I avoided flying, and, correspondingly, my self-confidence kept sinking. One day, I read an article in the newspaper about a fear-of-flying course and how to overcome such fear. Then and there, I decided to face this fear once and for all. I signed up for the course and made a commitment to myself to fly four to six times a year after that. The course helped, although I still felt somewhat anxious when flying for several years afterward. But I kept flying on a regular basis. Am I perfectly over my fear? No, not totally, but I fly in relative comfort — and feel more self-confident.

As you face and deal with specific fears, your self-confidence will grow and extend to other areas of life as well. New challenges and old obstacles in life can be approached with a greater measure of inner strength. The opposite is also true, however. If you do not face your fears, they grow and multiply, and your self-confidence begins to slip away. So it is important to face and come to terms with fears. In this regard, a useful exercise is to list some things you would like to do but have been putting off. After you have made your list, pick one thing you have some anxiety about, such as overcoming your fear of flying, starting a project you've been avoiding, or taking up a new hobby, and begin a program to do something about it. If you can do it on your own, then begin. If you feel you need professional help, get it. The important thing is to begin doing something about the problem rather than avoiding it or putting it off.

making your own decisions

As you find that you can spend time by yourself, live by your own values and face your fears, making your own decisions become easier. In terms of building your self-esteem, it's very important to be able to make your own decisions about matters that are important to you, whether these be minor problems or long-range goals. Problems develop when you become overly reliant or dependent on others, such as friends, family, parents, spouse, or experts, and let them make your decisions rather than making them yourself.

The more you let others decide what's right for you, the less likely you are to get what you want in any situation. One of the best ways of liking yourself is to make your own decision about a problem, take full responsibility for it, and be willing to live with the consequences. Very often the tendency is to assume that if *you* don't make the decision and let your spouse or an expert do it, then *they* are responsible if things don't work out. The truth is, however, that they are not responsible, and *you* are the one who suffers the consequences of the decision. Further, if your spouse or the expert were right and things do work out, then you can't take the credit and have the good feeling that goes with having made the "correct" decision. Either way you lose. To learn to love yourself, you have to be willing to make your own decisions and exercise your own independent judgement.

An exercise that can be useful in this regard is to try the following the next time you have a decision to make:

First, spend some time by yourself, analyzing the problem and deciding how you want to handle it. During this first stage, don't consult anyone else — just rely on yourself.

Second, after you have made up your *own* mind, if you wish you can now consult others and get their opinions. Remember, you are asking for their ideas, but not asking them to dictate what you should do.

Third, after you have their suggestions, make up your own mind, come to a decision and implement it.

Practicing this exercise repeatedly will help you trust your decision-making abilities more.

summary

There are two broad areas that need to be understood if you are to develop positive self-esteem: one, the attitudes that you hold toward yourself and two, your actual behavior. In terms of attitude, you need to look at and understand yourself in a realistic manner, not expecting too much from yourself. You also need to be willing to accept your mistakes and failures and learn from them, rather than being self-critical. In addition, you need to praise and reward yourself for the things that you do that are positive. You also need to develop behaviors which are consistent with your self-image; this will help you develop self-respect. You need to be willing to do things which you fear, thus developing self-confidence. You also need to be able to be alone and make your own decisions. Practicing these eight things will lead to the development of positive self-esteem.

In this chapter, we have also examined both the attitudes and behavior necessary to increase feelings of self-worth. Self-esteem is not something people are either blessed or cursed with, but rather something which can be developed by personal effort, and which can be increased by thought and action. In short, self-esteem for adults is not a gift but something they must work for and earn. Being successful in a love relationship is contingent upon loving yourself. One of the best methods of learning to accept and love yourself is to develop a sense of positive self-esteem. When you have done so, the quality of your love relationship will improve greatly.

conclusion

I have tried in this book to suggest some practical, workable ideas for helping couples build a more successful love relationship.

From my own clinical experience I have found that the major area most people neglect is what might be called a prerequisite to love: learning to love yourself. For that reason I have devoted the last two chapters of this book to how people can learn specifically to accept and love themselves more. Many people tend to rush into love relationships looking for someone else to build their self-esteem, make them happy, or help them overcome their personal problems. But love cannot flourish under such heavy responsibilities. Love works best when you develop your self-esteem yourself, and grow and develop as a person on your own.

In short, people need to grow up before they fall in love and get married or become involved in a long-term committed relationship. Otherwise they put too much of a burden on their loved ones. Learning to love yourself can take real discipline, but the rewards are substantial when you are successful. As a result you then can truly begin to love someone else.

We often tend to believe that love is easy — or should be, anyway. To excel at a career, to be a successful parent, to acquire a mastery of a sport, to play a musical instrument, however, are accomplishments which require discipline, work, time, commitment, and patience. To be successful in love is no different. Couples need to avoid the pitfalls of the self-defeating relationship and also need to work at communicating effectively, solving their differences, understanding their differing sexual natures, and becoming true friends. This book provides what I consider to be a blue print for building a good love relationship. A successful relationship will still require your commitment and hard work. But give it a try — I'm sure you'll find it's more than worth the effort!

index

description 84-85, 94
treatment 86-87, 96-97

– P –

Parent Role 79-81, 84-85

Passiveness 18, 45, 46-47, 59, 60, 76, 78, 82, 87, 89, 91-92, 97, 98

Personal-Emotional Acceptance 25, 30, 31, 32-33
definition 26
priority of need in men and women 26-29, 30, 35-36

Perfectionism 112, 115-116

Play-Fun Need 3, 4, 14, 53-54, 79-80, 87, 100, 104, 109-110, 112-113, 116, 121

Positive Attention 67-68

Power, balance of (See Balance of Power)

Praising Yourself 118-119, 123

Problem Solving (See Conflict Resolution)

Problems, identifying 49

Psychological Needs,
Basic (See Basic Psychological Needs)

– Q –

Qualitative Time 65-68

– R –

Relationship Need 4, 104, 105, 107-108, 109, 110, 111, 121

Resentment 8, 12, 18, 20, 34, 36, 41, 42, 74, 77, 83, 88, 89, 93, 94, 96, 97, 119

Resolving Differences 3, 13, 14, 39, 40, 41-44, 46-50, 75, 100, 125

Respect 23, 43, 44, 93, 94
loss of 22, 42, 76, 92, 107

Role Flexibility 78-80

Role Playing 55-56, 74

Role Rigidity 4, 78, 80-81, 100

Romantic Love 7-8, 9, 11, 13-14, 44, 57
difference from Mature Love 12-13

– S –

Security-Protection Need 33-34, 35, 36

Self-Acceptance 4, 54, 73-74, 104, 112, 113-114, 115-116, 117, 118, 119, 120, 123, 125

Self-Assessment of Psychological Needs 111-113
achievement need 112
autonomy-independence need 111-112
play-fun need 112-113
relationship need 111

Self-Concept (See also Self-Confidence, Self-Esteem)
negative 10
positive 10, 75, 109

Self-Confidence 83, 93, 94, 95, 97, 99, 100, 112, 119-120, 121-122, 123
loss of 77

Self-Criticism 115-116, 117, 123